Surprising
CITRUS

Surprising
CITRUS

A COOKBOOK

by
Audra & Jack Hendrickson

A Garden Way Publishing Book

STOREY

Storey Communications, Inc.
Schoolhouse Road
Pownal, Vermont 05261

Front cover photograph by Didier Delmas
Designed and produced by Nancy Lamb
Cover design & drawings on pages 124–138 by Wanda Harper
Edited by Constance Oxley

Typesetting by Hemmings Publishing
Printed in the United States by Alpine Press

Snacker® is a trademark of Sunkist Growers, Inc.,
  Los Angeles, California.

First printing, July 1988

Library of Congress Catalog Card Number: 87-04644
International Standard Book Number: 0-88266-515-4 (pb)
                                    0-88266-514-6 (hc)
Library of Congress Cataloging-in-Publication Data

Hendrickson, Audra.
        Surprising citrus.

        "A Garden Way Publishing book."
        Includes index.
        1. Cookery (Citrus fruits) I. Hendrickson, Jack.
II. Title.
TX813.C5H46 1988 641.6'435   87-46444
ISBN 0-88266-514-6
ISBN 0-88266-515-4 (pbk.)

*This book is dedicated to our parents and
our grandparents and all those
who came before us.*

CONTENTS

Food for Thought............................... 1
Kinds of Citrus 3
Facts About Citrus 6
Cook's Helpers................................ 9
Appetizers & Snacks 13
Beverages................................... 21
Breakfast & Brunch 33
Salads & Dressings........................... 39
Entrées & Sauces 49
Soups & Side Dishes 63
Breads 73
Desserts:
    Cakes, Tortes, Cookies & Bars............. 81
    Fillings, Toppings, Ices & Creams 93
    Pies, Pastries & Puddings 103
Marmalades & More.......................... 111
How to Buy Citrus Fruits 121
How to Store Citrus Fruits.................... 122
Tools for Citrus Artistry 124
Special Citrus Techniques 128
Special Citrus Treatments 133
Appendices 139
Index 143

FOOD FOR THOUGHT

One of the most controversial of all the vitamins as far as disease prevention is concerned is vitamin C, the food element better known to science as ascorbic acid. A water-soluble nutrient, it is found in its natural state in many fruits and vegetables. Oranges, lemons, grapefruit, limes, mandarins or tangerines, and other citrus fruits are among the richest natural sources of vitamin C. A single four-ounce glass of orange juice provides roughly 100 percent of the Recommended Daily Dietary Allowance (see Table I page 139).

Scientists have determined that vitamin C is essential to the formation of collagen, an elastic protein substance needed to bind skin cells together and give tone and smoothness to the complexion. It is required for healthy cartilage, bones, teeth, and tissue metabolism. Vitamin C aids in the absorption of iron which builds up capillary strength for better circulation, the prevention of bruising, and the promotion of healing. It stimulates production of white blood cells which protect the body against infections and bacterial toxins. Many believe — along with the late Nobel prize winner, Dr. Linus Pauling — that vitamin C wards off the common cold, and that massive doses help protect against some cancers.

The committee of experts which compiled the National Research Council's massive 1982 report, "Diet, Nutrition and Cancer," concluded — based on the results of many studies — that *vitamin C can inhibit the formation of some carcinogens, and that consumption of vitamin C-containing foods is associated with a lower risk . . . for certain* cancers, particularly *gastric and esophogeal cancer."* An inhibitive effect on laryngeal cancer was found in one study, and researchers showed that diets rich in vitamin C might be responsible for curtailing development of uterine cervical displasia.

Approximately one out of 20 new cancer cases, and one out of 17 cancer-caused deaths is from cancer of the esophagus, stomach or larynx.

Such epidemiological evidence suggests that the food choices we make may cause us to develop cancer or *they may save us from cancer.* Some medical researchers estimate that improper diet is the cause of 30 to 40 percent of cancers in men and up to 60 percent of those in women. Many other ailments are known to be brought on or aggravated by diet, including stroke and diseases of the heart, kidneys, and liver.

Citrus fruits have unusually great "nutrient density" — the proportion of nutrients to calories — and nutritionists tell us we need about 40 different kinds of nutrients daily to maintain good health.

Small amounts of the many B-complex vitamins are found in citrus fruits, including thiamine, riboflavin, niacin, pantothenic acid, B_6, folacin, and B_{12}. A minute quantity of biotin is also present. Thiamine and pantothenic acid are needed for carbohydrate metabolism and conversion of other foods into energy. Riboflavin and niacin help regulate metabolism and promote healthy skin. Vitamin B_6, folacin, and B_{12} are essential to the formation of red blood cells (see Table II page 140).

Citrus fruits also contain small but important quantities of nutrients such as beta-carotene, the precursor of vitamin A (see *THE CARROT COOK-BOOK*, pages 7-9); plus calcium, phosphorous, potassium, iron, and trace amounts of magnesium, zinc, copper, and manganese. Potassium is particularly important to the maintenance of health. It is lost in exercise or due to stress associated with hypertension. Orange juice ranks high among foods as a source of natural potassium — a fact which should be of particular interest to readers who need potassium but have found they experience nausea when they take synthetic potassium supplements. (See Table III page 141.)

In addition to the nutrients they contain, citrus fruits are high in fiber, an indigestible but very necessary part of the foods we eat. Not only does citrus pulp contain fiber, but the white inside surface of the rind — the albedo — is especially rich in fiber. Most medical experts believe that fiber greatly assists in the regular elimination of digestive wastes. Some theorize that fiber helps to prevent diabetes and gastrointestinal disorders such as diverticular disease, diarrhea, and colon cancer.

Worldwide, populations with diets containing twice as much fiber as in American diets — on average, we eat only about 10 to 20 grams per day — have a significantly lower rate of rectal and colon cancers than do U.S. citizens. The National Cancer Institute recommends we eat foods providing from 25 to 35 grams of fiber daily.

Citrus fruits, especially when peeled so as not to remove all the albedo, are outstanding sources of the fiber our bodies require for good health.

Avoiding the *wrong* foods is just as important as eating the *right* ones. According to the National Research Council, most Americans include too much fat in their daily diets in spite of evidence showing its dangers to health. They recommend that people cut fat intake to no more than 30 percent of their daily calories from the 40 percent that is the average now.

Citrus fruits are almost totally free of fat. Like most fruits, they are largely composed of carbohydrates, with a modest amount of protein matter and a trace of — or *no* — fat. In terms of calories, members of the citrus family are uniformly on the low side (see Table IV page 142).

They are also extremely low in sodium. High sodium intake has been identified by medical experts as one of several factors believed to be associated with hypertension, or high blood pressure. It is estimated by the National Institute of Health that about 60 million Americans have some degree of hypertension. Untreated, it can lead to heart attack, stroke, and kidney disease.

Nutritionists tell us we can get adequate sodium from natural foods and water without ever lifting a salt shaker over our plates or saucepans. Fortunately for all of us who like good food and want to stay healthy, the abundance and availability of citrus fruits make it unnecessary to choose between good taste and good health. Citrus fruits are nature's most versatile low-sodium flavor enhancers, with so little sodium it is difficult to find enough to measure (see Table III page 141). Yet they enhance the flavors of other foods just as salt does.

Instead of shaking on salt, we can squeeze on lemon or lime juice. A full cup of either has only two tiny milligrams of sodium. A medium orange and half a grapefruit contain barely a trace of sodium each, and a cup of their juice, only two. In contrast, one teaspoon of table salt contains over 2000 milligrams of sodium. *It would take mountains of grapefruit and oranges or a thousand cups of citrus juice to add up to the sodium in just one teaspoon of table salt.*

In addition to being virtually fat- and sodium-free, citrus fruits contain *no* cholesterol. Quite the opposite: Albedo pectin has been found to *reduce* cholesterol in the blood by a "small but significant" amount.

Based on information such as that given above, professionals in the fields of diet, nutrition, and health recommend that you:

1. Include a variety of fresh fruits and vegetables plus a generous amount of whole grain foods in your diet;
2. Control your weight by cutting down on fat, both saturated and unsaturated;
3. Minimize your use of sugar, sodium, and salt; and
4. Drink alcohol sparingly or not at all.

You should also adhere to the Recommended Daily Dietary Allowance (RDA) guidelines compiled by the nutrition professionals of the U.S. Food and Drug Administration. (See Table I page 139.)

Though citrus fruits and citrus products cannot completely satisfy Recommended Daily Dietary Allowance requirements, they can supply a significant portion of them. But, it is important to remember that the body does not store vitamin C: A new supply must be taken in *every day.*

The recipes that follow have been compiled, developed, and tested to make getting your daily supply of vitamin C both easy and enjoyable. They range from *Saucy Baked Chicken* to *Frozen Calico Cream,* from *Sunday Punch* to *Omelette Orange,* from *Key Lime Pie* to *Cartwheels MacMuffin* — with dozen of delicious others in between.

¡Salud comida y bebida y tiempo para gozarlas!
Audra and Jack Hendrickson

KINDS OF CITRUS FRUITS

Before the middle of this century, one investigator reported that nearly 100 varieties of orange alone had been developed and were being cultivated in various parts of the world. Today that number is even larger, and there are dozens of varieties of other citrus fruits, as well. However, we have found that there are eleven basic, commercially produced types of citrus fruit to choose from in the produce bins at our supermarkets or grocery stores: Sweet oranges, sour oranges, grapefruit, pummelos, lemons, limes, mandarins (tangerines), kumquats, tangelos, tangors, and citrons.

Each type has its own family of varieties developed by horticulturists in their never-ending search for improved taste, greater juice content, better color, and staggered harvest times. Experimentation has also increased resistance to frost, disease and pest damage, ease of cultivating and harvesting, and storage time.

Sweet Oranges

Washington navels and Valencias are perhaps the most familiar varieties of orange on the U.S. market, most of them grown in Florida and California. The navel — named for the dimple at the bottom tip of the fruit — is also recognized by its distinctive pebbled rind. It is of medium size, sweet, seedless, easy to peel, nicely sectioned, and well suited to snacking or use in prepared dishes.

Like the navel, the Valencia is sweet and neatly sectioned. The fruit is round to slightly globular in shape, medium-to-large in size. Its thinner rind is smooth or only slightly pebbled. The fruit is nearly seedless and very juicy, making it the so-called "king of the juice oranges."

The other major sweet orange varieties include Hamlin, Parson Brown, Marrs, Diller, and Pineapple.

The Hamlin is sweet and juicy, a medium-small orange with a smooth, thin peel, usually seedless. It originated in Florida and is grown there as well as in Texas, California, and in the Gulf states. In Arizona, it is grown and marketed as an "Arizona Sweet."

The Parson Brown is sweet and juicy, medium-to-large size, oblong in shape with smooth, bright, yellowish rind. Florida grown, it is also cultivated in Texas, Arizona, and Louisiana.

Marrs, Pineapple, and Diller are small-to-medium oranges, relatively seedy, sweet and juicy, all grown primarily in Arizona where they are also known as Arizona Sweets.

Sour Oranges

The best known sour orange is the Spanish Seville (pronounced Sev-ill in England where it is *the* ingredient in proper British marmalade.) Along with Chinotto and Bouquet — two other variations of the sour orange — the Seville is aromatic, quite bitter, and not widely popular here or abroad for anything *except* marmalade.

Grapefruit

The major grapefruit varieties, all of which are from 3½-5 inches in diameter, are the medium-to-large white-fleshed Duncan, with a thick smooth rind, excellent flavor, and seeds; and the medium-to-large Marsh Seedless, characterized by a smooth thin rind, good flavor and few, if any, seeds.

Pink– or red-fleshed varieties have been developed from both the Marsh and the Duncan: The medium-large Thompson (Pink Marsh), Ruby Red, and Redblush, having medium-smooth rinds and few-to-many seeds, from the Marsh; Foster and Star Ruby from the Duncan.

Pummelo

The pummelo, or pomelo, is the progenitor of the modern grapefruit and a close relative of the citron. Similar in appearance to the grapefruit, it is much larger, egg-shaped, with a tart, distinctive flavor. Two varieties are most readily available in American markets: Chandler and Reinking. The pink-fleshed Chandler has a sugary-acid flavor and is moderately juicy. Reinking flesh closely resembles that of a standard grapefruit: It tastes like the Chandler.

Lemons

Virtually all lemons grown in this country are the acid type. A small number of sweet lemons are produced, but not commercially. The two principal varieties of acid lemon are the Eureka and the Lisbon.

The native California Eureka is sometimes egg shaped, often distinctively oblong, with a short neck at the stem end and a prominent nipple at the blossom end. The skin is slightly ridged. The neck and nipple of the Lisbon, which originated in Portugal, are less prominent and the skin is smoother than the Eureka. Both varieties are highly acid and juicy, with few or no seeds.

Limes

These cousins of lemons resemble their kin in shape and acidic nature though not in size or color. The two main varieties are: The large, practically seedless, yellowish-fruited lime called Tahiti or Persian in Florida but known as Bearss (sic) in California; and the smaller seeded Mexican or Key lime with dark green fruit and rind which is known as the West Indian lime in Florida and the bartender's lime in California.

Mandarins

These fruits are often thought to be tangerines, but most experts say the opposite is true. What most of us know as the tangerine is a mandarin variety called the Dancy.

The Clementine and Dancy are probably the best known and most popular mandarins in America. They are medium in size, have a thin rind, orange-red flesh, and a medium number of seeds. Both feature the familiar loose peeling that led Col. G.L. Dancy, an early Florida grower, to call it the "kid glove" orange.

All mandarin varieties feature that easy peeling and are also neatly sectioned, rich in flavor, and very juicy.

Kumquats

Kumquats (pronounced *come-kwats*) are small fruits about the size and shape of unshelled almonds. A fully ripe kumquat has two or three seeds, and a skin that is tangy, sweet, and edible, with juicy pulp inside. There are two popular varieties: Meiwa and Nagami.

Tangelos

There are four principal varieties of the tangelo, which is a cross between either a mandarin and a grapefruit or a mandarin and a pummelo: Minneola, a large, round, orange-red fruit with a thin, finely pitted rind and a characteristic "neck" at the stem end, few seeds, and a rich tart taste; the medium-large, orange-red Orlando with a taste that is mildly sweet and mandarin-like, rather seedy; the large, yellow-orange Sampson which looks and tastes much like a grapefruit, with many seeds; and the medium-large, red-orange Seminole, a rather seedy fruit with tart flesh.

Tangors

The tangor, frequently called the "Temple Orange" and sometimes the "Royal Mandarin," is a hybrid, a cross between a mandarin and an orange, with many of the best qualities of each parent. The Temple is a rather large, plump fruit, red-orange in color with a loose rind that is easy to peel, its pulp spicy and fairly juicy. The Dweet is also red-orange in color, somewhat smaller, and egg shaped, with a barely perceptible "neck." Its fruit is sweet, slightly tart, and very juicy.

Citron

The Citron is a fruit that isn't — at least it's nothing like — a typical fruit. Its skimpy pulp is dry, full of seeds, sour, acidic, tough, and hard to get at through its thick rind. In fact, it's the rind of the citron that makes it worthwhile. Its distinctive aromatic quality was prized by ancients of the Middle East and Rome. The oil of the rind — or flavedo — was used to keep dwellings and clothing fragrant; the white inner part of the rind — or albedo — was a favorite salad ingredient; bits of the whole rind were combined with spices to make a sauce for fish. Today, it is most often candied and used to add flavor to baked goods.

When the citron is available as a whole fruit, it will likely be the Etrog or the Fingered citron — sometimes called Buddha's Hand — named for its distinctive shape, which resembles the drooping fingers of a human hand.

FACTS ABOUT CITRUS FRUITS

Citrus fruits and their by-products are present in scores of consumables that we see and use everyday — juices, slushes, marmalades, molasses, syrups, wines, alcohol, and candied and jellied products. They are bases for such products as perfumes, soaps, cosmetics, pharmaceuticals, paints, insecticides, rubber, textiles, confections, and ice creams. Orange, lemon, and lime are the three most popular citrus flavors and colors in food manufacturing.

Vitamin C is protected during citrus juice freezing by the fruits' own supplies of citric acid.

You can conserve the abundant vitamin C content of citrus fruits by storing them in a cold or cool place and by not peeling or slicing them until just before you use them. After peeling, cutting, grating or shredding the fruits, refrigerate them until served.

Vitamin C is water-soluble. If the citrus fruit you are preparing requires washing after peeling, do it quickly. Other vitamins such as those of the B-complex, sugars, flavinols, and minerals may also be leached away during soaking.

In addition to being an important source of vitamin C, citrus fruits of all kinds supply varying amounts of beta-carotene, thiamine, riboflavin, and niacin, plus vital minerals such as calcium, phosphorus, iron, and potassium, with only slight traces of sodium.

Studies show that people who gradually cut down on salt soon lose their craving for it. Citrus juice is a good substitute for high-sodium table salt.

Growers tell us that a green tinge on oranges doesn't mean they're "green," or not ripe. The fruits require both warm days and cool nights to achieve their characteristic bright orange color. If nights are too warm as they develop, the oranges ripen but retain some green color. Thus, certifiably ripe oranges can stay green until cool weather arrives to turn them orange.

Ripe Florida oranges are sometimes artificially colored. The process, called "degreening," is regulated by the federal Food and Drug Administration to assure that the oranges we buy are mature and that the coloring agent used is harmless.

Orange juice is a source of folic acid (folacin), a compound important in the diet of pregnant women and those taking oral contraceptives. A six-ounce serving daily helps to combat the anemia associated with folic acid deficiency.

Orange peel can contain more vitamin C than any other part of the fruit. However, even without its peel, one medium orange supplies about 66 mg of vitamin C, 110 percent of the Recommended Daily Dietary Allowance for adults. Oranges should be kept in the refrigerator in order to conserve their vitamin C.

The albedo of an orange — the white pith just under the peel — is a rich source of the pectin fiber that is helpful in reducing serum cholesterol levels.

Oranges are high in dietary fiber, low in calories — only 60 in the average fruit — and they have practically no sodium. They are rich in potassium and beta-carotene. The average fruit has 16 grams of carbohydrates.

Oranges and mandarins (such as tangerines) are naturally high in sugar content. At least one state has gone so far as to *prohibit* the addition of sugar — or anything else — to frozen orange juice concentrate.

The stacked cans of juice produced each year in Florida would reach from the earth to the moon. Laid end to end, they would circle the globe nine times.

The pectin in grapefruit helps reduce serum cholesterol, and just half of one fruit supplies up to 60 percent of the National Academy of Science's Recommended Daily Dietary Allowance of vitamin C for adults, 100 milligrams of potassium, a trace of sodium, few calories, and practically no fat.

Half or more of U.S. grapefruit production is processed into canned and frozen concentrated juices.

Grapefruit do not ripen after picking because they contain very little starch for conversion into sugar. Their quality deteriorates with age: The longer the storage period, the greater the loss of juice and flavor.

Pink or red grapefruit contain a generous supply of vitamin A as well as vitamin C — up to 600 International Units or over 10 percent of the National Academy of Science's Recommended Daily Dietary Allowance for adults in each whole fruit. The vitamin A is in the form of beta-carotene, which accounts for the pink or reddish color of the pulp and juice.

Pummelos, which taste like sweet grapefruit, ripen with much less heat than grapefruit, coming to market fresh even in December.

Lemons that are ideal market size and dark green when harvested have the longest storage life. They are picked "green" in order to preserve their acidic content, when their juice content reaches at least 42 percent. They have a higher percentage of thirst-quenching citric acid than any other fruit.

The lemon blossom, symbolizing fidelity, is the birthday flower for those born on January 12th.

The juice of one 2-inch diameter lemon provides 31 milligrams of vitamin C or 51 percent of the National Academy of Sciences Recommended Daily Dietary Allowance for adults. One cup of lemon juice has only 60 calories.

Lime trees, like lemon trees, may blossom almost the year-round. The juice content of their fruit increases after picking and during storage, and averages about 65 calories per cup.

Limes are high in ascorbic acid (vitamin C) content: A medium lime contains 25 milligrams. They also have generous amounts of potassium and beta-carotene.

Mandarins are excellent sources of ascorbic acid (vitamin C): One fruit provides nearly 40 percent of the NRC Recommended Daily Dietary Allowance. They also contain phosphorus, potassium, beta-carotene, and iron, and are low in sodium and fat, with only 34 calories in a medium-size fruit.

One large tangerine has about 50 calories, 2 milligrams of sodium, half the vitamin C recommended daily for adults, and a good share of the body's daily potassium needs.

Harvested from December through May, kumquats have a sweet edible skin and tangy flesh and can be eaten whole, except for the seeds. Like all other citrus fruits, they are a good source of vitamin C and beta-carotene. They also supply generous portions of minerals such as calcium, magnesium, phosphorous, and potassium. In addition, they are low in calories and sodium, and contain no measurable fat or cholesterol.

Citron's pungent flavor has led to the development of the candied citron peel found in most supermarkets. While production of candied citron peel is a flourishing industry, citron is not widely distributed as an unprocessed fruit.

COOK'S HELPERS

Citrus rind is rich in vitamins and minerals — both the *flavedo* or thin, colored outer skin, and the *albedo*, the white layer of pith that forms the inner surface of the rind. In this book, *rind* will refer to the entire covering of the fruit, including both flavedo and albedo; *peel* will refer to the flavedo only; and *zest* will refer to scrapings from the very outer surface of the flavedo.

Never use tools and utensils containing copper when cooking or serving citrus dishes, since copper quickly and completely destroys vitamin C.

Avoid overcooking and high-heat cooking in order to retain the maximum amount of vitamin C. Whenever possible, add citrus ingredients *after* the cooking is completed; bring other ingredients to the boiling point *before* adding citrus fruits. Cover pans with tight-fitting lids to preserve even more vitamin C.

Squeeze several drops of fresh citrus juice into the cooking water of white vegetables such as cauliflower or potatoes, and dip celery into lemon-water to help prevent discoloring.

Make a citrus "tree" for an unusual centerpiece by stacking alternate cartwheels of grapefruit, orange, lemon, lime, and kumquat on a plate and topping the pyramid with an ornament.

At Hallowe'en time, carve large oranges, grapefruit, and pummelos like pumpkins; scoop out the pulp and membrane and anchor a small birthday candle in each fruit.

If all you need is a few drops of lemon or lime juice, roll the fruit to soften it, push a toothpick deep into it, withdraw the toothpick, and squeeze out as much juice as you need. Replace the toothpick as a "stopper" and store the fruit in the refrigerator.

When a beverage or drink calls for a twist of lemon peel, give the peel a sharp twist in order to release the pungent oils contained in the flavedo.

Make your own sour or buttermilk from homogenized "regular" milk by adding a tablespoon of lemon juice per cup. Let it sit for five minutes before using.

For a quick and delicious ice cream topping, warm ½ cup thick chocolate syrup with ¼ cup lime juice.

Mix applesauce with a selection of citrus pieces. Sprinkle with nutmeg and chopped nuts.

Thinly slice whole oranges and arrange the slices in layers in a bowl, sugaring each layer. Pour your favorite liqueur over the orange slices and chill overnight. Serve cold.

Make a lemonade or limeade slush by combining lemon or lime juice with sugar, water, and ice cubes and blending until smooth.

Float thin lemon slices in all kinds of vegetable soups, and in beef, chicken or tomato bouillon.

Cut whole oranges horizontally into ½-inch slices, insert wooden fudgesicle sticks into them, arrange on waxed paper or foil, and freeze. When frozen solid, put them into airtight bags for storage in the freezer. They make delicious hot weather treats for youngsters and grown-ups.

Arrange trimmed grapefruit sections spiral fashion on a large plate and drizzle warm honey over them, sprinkle with coconut, chill, and serve.

Make a citrus milkshake by blending trimmed sections of orange or tangerine with a half cup of milk and a pint of vanilla ice cream.

Wash and dry fresh kumquats, remove the stem ends, and trim off any blemishes. Cut the fruits in halves, remove all seeds, and stuff the halves with softened cream cheese.

One medium orange contains 10-11 sections, about 5 teaspoons of grated peel, ⅔ cup of combined pulp and juice, ½ cup of bite-sized pieces and ⅓-½ cup of juice.

One medium grapefruit contains 6-8 ounces of juice, 10-12 sections, 1-1½ cups of bite-sized pieces, and 3-5 tablespoons of grated peel.

One medium lemon contains ¼-⅓ cup of juice and 3-4 teaspoons of grated peel, and a medium tangerine contains ½ cup of sections.

After serving finger-foods, provide guests with bowls filled with warm water and a slice of lemon.

Place bowls of lemons around the house to keep it smelling fresh and clean, and put reamed-out lemon shells down the garbage disposer.

Remove odors from hands or pots and pans used to prepare fish by rubbing them with a piece of cut lemon just before washing.

We have found that the best way to grate the peel of a tangerine is to remove the rind in quarter sections from the fruit, anchor one end of it orange side up on a flat surface, and pull the grater over the peel. The peel can also be ground up in a food grinder or processor. Simply remove the peel from the fruit, cut into small pieces, and grind or process it to the fineness you want.

Citrus peel can be dried by placing strips of it in a warm and airy place, such as over a stove or on top of a refrigerator. Let the peel dry naturally and completely. When you are ready to use the peel, place in cold water, and boil in a covered saucepan until soft.

Once you've used the pulp from citrus halves, scrape out as much of the white membrane as you can without piercing the shell; fill the halves with ice cream or sherbet, mashed sweet potatoes, mixed fruits folded into whipped cream, bite-sized pieces of oranges, grapefruit, mandarins, and kumquats, tapioca or rice pudding.

Make pomander balls by studding whole oranges or lemons as thickly as possible with whole cloves. Tie bright ribbon around the balls and hang them in closets to keep the closets smelling sweet and fresh.

Citrus rind is rich in vitamins and minerals. Conserve and use the "flavedo" of orange, lemon, lime, and grapefruit peel — the thin, brightly colored outer skin — instead of artificial flavorings. The tiny oil sacs that it contains are full of subtle and distinctive flavor that gives sauces, frostings, baked goods, puddings, and beverages a wonderful fresh taste.

Pummelo varieties are often less sweet and less juicy than grapefruit so they are not usually eaten on the "half-shell" as standard breakfast fare. Peeled and sectioned, they are good as finger-foods or combined with other fruits in salads and on snack trays.

Citrus juice is nature's best salt substitute for those on sodium-restricted diets.

Squeeze a little fresh lemon juice into the final rinse water when you shampoo your hair. It will be squeaky clean, fragrant, and shiny.

Bouncy bright green limes have a sharp citrus flavor that makes them unequaled for adding piquancy to every kind of dish. Grate the peel into vegetables, seafood, and meat entrées, and use it to flavor drinks, punches, sherbets, puddings, and baked goods.

Packed with vitamin C, 1 ounce of fresh lime juice has only 8 calories.

Contrary to popular belief, the vitamin C in citrus fruits does not deteriorate rapidly during storage. Fresh fruits contain a substance which inhibits vitamin C oxidation — the same substance that does the job when we squeeze fresh citrus juice on pears, apples or bananas to keep them from discoloring. In fact, fresh citrus loses very little of its vitamin C value during shipping, selling or home storage.

Snack-Time Dips

These dips take only minutes to prepare once you have the ingredients assembled and at room temperature. The directions for making all of them are the same: Blend or beat the ingredients together in a medium mixing bowl. Yields will vary from 1½–2 cups. Serve with chips, fruits, raw vegetables or crackers.

I.   3 tablespoons lemon juice
    1 8-ounce package cream cheese, softened
    1 teaspoon minced onion
    1 teaspoon salt
    dash Worcestershire sauce
    1 cup mashed avocado

II.   6 hard-cooked eggs
    ¼ cup *LEMONNAISE* (see page 45)
    ¼ cup low-fat yogurt
    2 tablespoons lemon juice
    dash garlic powder
    dash Worcestershire sauce
    dash Tabasco sauce
    salt and pepper to taste

III.   ⅓ cup milk
    1 8-ounce package cream cheese, softened
    2 teaspoons lemon juice
    ¼ teaspoon onion juice
    dash Worcestershire sauce
    ¾ cup cooked shrimp

IV.   ¼ cup sour cream
    1 8-ounce package cream cheese, softened
    ¼ cup creamed horseradish

    2 tablespoons minced parsley
    4 teaspoons lemon juice
    1 tablespoon grated onion

V.   1 avocado, peeled and mashed
    1 tomato, chopped
    1 tablespoon lemon juice
    1 teaspoon Worcestershire sauce
    ½ teaspoon salt, or to taste
    1 small onion, minced

VI.   ½ cup lemon-flavored yogurt
    ½ cup sour cream
    1 tablespoon honey
    ½ cup grapefruit juice

VII.   1 cup sour cream
    1 tablespoon honey
    ½ cup orange juice
    1 tablespoon lemon juice

VIII.   1 avocado, mashed
    ⅛ cup lemon juice
    dash onion juice
    dash salt
    dash pepper

Spreads and Fillings

Have all the ingredients assembled and at room temperature before you start to prepare these spreads and fillings. Then combine them in the order in which the ingredients are listed. Yields will vary from 1½–2 cups. Spread them on crackers, sandwich breads or toast rounds.

I.
½ cup *MIXED CITRUS MARMALADE*
   (see page 113)
1 3-ounce package cream cheese, softened
¼ cup chopped nuts

II.
1 tablespoon orange juice
1 teaspoon orange zest
½ cup crunchy peanut butter
½ cup cream cheese, softened

III.
1 cup low-fat cottage cheese
1 3-ounce package cream cheese, softened
1 teaspoon lemon juice
1 teaspoon lemon zest
½ cup bite-sized orange pieces
2 tablespoons chopped nuts

Mixed Fruit Cup

PREPARATION TIME: 10-15 MINUTES
CHILLING TIME: 1-2 HOURS
YIELD: 4-6 SERVINGS

1 cup mandarin sections
1 cup pineapple chunks, with juice
½ cup seedless grapes
½ cup shredded coconut
mint leaves

Combine the fruits and the coconut in a medium mixing bowl, tossing together gently.

Chill covered for 1–2 hours. Garnish with the mint leaves and serve.

Pink Cocktail

1 pink grapefruit
1 cup cooked shrimp
⅓ cup chili sauce
⅓ cup low-fat cottage cheese
1 teaspoon lemon juice
4 lemon wedges
parsley sprigs

Peel and section the grapefruit (see page 129). Remove the membrane between the sections.

Cut the sections into bite-sized pieces and combine with the shrimp in a medium mixing bowl. Spoon the grapefruit mixture evenly into four cocktail dishes.

Combine the chili sauce with the cottage cheese and the lemon juice in a blender or processor and blend until smooth.

Pour this pink sauce equally over the grapefruit and shrimp in the cocktail dishes. Garnish each serving with a lemon wedge and a parsley sprig and serve.

Grapefruit on the Half Shell

2 pink grapefruit
4 tablespoons *LOVERS' MARMALADE*
  (see page 112)

Preheat the broiler and have the broiler tray ready.

Cut the grapefruit in half. Loosen the sections by cutting around each with a curved grapefruit knife (see page 126). Snip out the center cores with kitchen shears.

Top each prepared grapefruit half with a tablespoon of *LOVERS' MARMALADE* and place the halves on the broiler tray.

Place the broiler tray on the broiler rack so the tops of the grapefruit are 3-5 inches from the heating element. Broil the fruits for about 5 minutes or until hot and bubbly. Serve.

Fresh Fruit Fondue

PREPARATION TIME: 15-20 MINUTES
CHILLING TIME: 2-4 HOURS
YIELD: 4-6 SERVINGS

Kim Leffler tried this recipe for us, and said her family loved it the first time around — and the second time, too. "I mixed a little LEMONNAISE *with the leftover* FONDUE *and folded in the leftover fruits. Served over lettuce, it made a nice next-day fruit salad."*

1 egg
2 tablespoons butter or margarine, softened
2 tablespoons brown sugar
1 teaspoon cornstarch
1 teaspoon orange zest
1 teaspoon lemon zest
1 cup orange juice

Combine all the ingredients in a blender and puree.

Turn the mixture into a small saucepan and cook, stirring constantly, until thick and smooth. Cool to room temperature.

Put into a covered glass or plastic container and chill.

Serve with a variety of fresh fruits cut into bite-sized pieces.

Pink Ladies

PREPARATION TIME: 10-15 MINUTES
CHILLING TIME: 2 HOURS
YIELD: 4-6 SERVINGS

2 pink grapefruit
½ cup powdered sugar
1 cup melon balls
¼ cup white zinfandel wine
½ cup pecan halves
½ cup shredded coconut

Working over a bowl in order not to waste any of the juice, peel, trim, and section the grapefruit, removing the membrane between the sections. Cut the sections into bite-sized pieces and sprinkle with the powdered sugar.

Form the melon balls and add to the grapefruit, along with the wine. Chill for at least 2 hours.

When ready to serve, fold in the pecans and the coconut.

Chilled Spiced Fruit

PREPARATION TIME: 45-60 MINUTES
CHILLING TIME: 2-4 HOURS
YIELD: 6-8 SERVINGS

1½ cups water
1 tablespoon tapioca
¼ teaspoon salt, or to taste
1½ cups mixed dried fruits
½ cup raisins
⅓ cup sugar
1 cinnamon stick
6 whole cloves
1 cup orange juice

Bring the water to a boil in a medium-large covered saucepan. Stir in the tapioca and the salt.

Cut the mixed fruits into small pieces and add, with the raisins, to the saucepan. Stir in the sugar, the cinnamon stick, and the cloves and cook over low heat, covered, until the fruits are tender, about 30-40 minutes.

Remove the cinnamon stick and the cloves and stir in the orange juice. Cool the fruits to room temperature. Chill for at least 2 hours before serving.

Broiled Grapefruit

PREPARATION TIME: 15 MINUTES
YIELD: 4 SERVINGS

2 grapefruit
8 teaspoons brown sugar
8 teaspoons kirsch
4 maraschino cherries

Preheat the broiler and have the broiler tray ready.

Halve the grapefruit, loosen the sections with a curved grapefruit knife, and remove the core and seeds.

Place the prepared grapefruit halves on the broiler tray and on each put 2 teaspoons of the brown sugar and 2 teaspoons of the kirsch. Place a cherry in the center of each half.

Set the broiler tray so the tops of the grapefruit are 3-5 inches from the heating element. Broil the fruits until hot and bubbly. Remove from the broiler and serve.

Grapefruit Puffs

PREPARATION TIME: 10-15 MINUTES
YIELD: 4 SERVINGS

2 grapefruit
¼ cup honey
¾ cup cherry pie filling
1 tablespoon orange zest
½ cup heavy cream

Cut the grapefruit in half and remove the cores. Cut around the outside and around each section to loosen it. Scoop out the loosened sections, remove the membrane that separates them, and put the trimmed fruit pieces into a large mixing bowl. Set aside.

Arrange the grapefruit shells on a serving platter and set aside.

Add the honey, the pie filling, and the orange zest to the reserved grapefruit pieces, blending thoroughly.

Whip the heavy cream until it stands in stiff peaks. Fold through the filling mixture.

Spoon the mixture equally into the reserved grapefruit shells and serve.

Seafood and Citrus Nests

PREPARATION TIME: 15-20 MINUTES
YIELD: 4 SERVINGS

¼ cup chili sauce
½ teaspoon minced green onion
½ teaspoon Worcestershire sauce
2 grapefruit
lettuce, shredded
1 6½-ounce can shredded crab meat, drained
parsley

In a blender, combine the chili sauce, the onion, and the Worcestershire sauce and puree. Set aside.

Cut the grapefruit in half. Remove the sections with a serrated grapefruit spoon over a bowl so that none of the juice is lost. Remove the membrane that separates the sections and all the membrane from the grapefruit shells and make a nest in each with the shredded lettuce.

Combine the crab meat with the grapefruit sections and their juice, along with the reserved chili sauce puree. Toss together gently.

Spoon the crab mixture into the grapefruit shells, garnish with the parsley, and serve.

Ambrosia Olympia

PREPARATION TIME: 10-15 MINUTES
CHILLING TIME: 2-4 HOURS
YIELD: 4-6 SERVINGS

Ambrosia was everyday fare for the gods and goddesses who lived on Mount Olympus in the good old days. Ambrosia was their food and nectar was their drink. Eon in and eon out. Yet they never complained about mealtime monotony. If the dish they were served tasted anything like this version, we can understand why.

4 oranges
1 cup shredded coconut
1 cup apricots, fresh or canned
1 cup low-fat cottage cheese
4 tablespoons honey
2 teaspoons orange zest
½ cup finely chopped pecans

Peel the oranges deeply enough to remove all of the white albedo. Cut the sections away from the membrane and remove the seeds. Cut the sections into bite-sized pieces (see page 130).

Arrange the orange pieces in a serving dish and sprinkle the coconut over them. Chop the apricots coarsely and spread over the coconut.

Combine the cottage cheese, the honey, and the orange zest in a blender or processor and puree. Pour the puree over the other ingredients in the serving dish, cover, and chill. Before serving, sprinkle with the pecans.

Cartwheels and Cream Cheese

PREPARATION TIME: 5-10 MINUTES
YIELD: 4 SERVINGS

4 oranges
1 3-ounce package cream cheese, softened
2 tablespoons Galliano liqueur
1 teaspoon orange zest
lettuce

Peel the oranges deeply to remove all of the white albedo. Cut the oranges into thick cartwheel slices (see page 132), reserving eight of the largest and best. Put the remaining slices aside for some other use.

Combine the cream cheese, the Galliano, and the orange zest in a small mixing bowl and blend together well.

Spread all of the cream cheese mixture thickly on four of the orange cartwheels. Place another orange cartwheel on top of the cream cheese mixture.

Arrange a bed of crisp lettuce on a serving plate or individual plates, add the cartwheels and cream cheese, and serve.

Glogg

Glogg is the traditional Christmas holiday drink for everyone who has even a drop of Swedish blood in his veins. In Sweden, they take their Glogg seriously. A large batch is often prepared long before the holidays in order to give it a chance to "ripen." The finished product is a powerful, delicious concoction that definitely packs a wallop.

1 fifth dry red wine
1 fifth muscatel wine
1 cup sweet vermouth
6 whole cardamoms, crushed
5 whole cloves
2 cinnamon sticks
1 cup raisins
peel of half an orange
¾ cup sugar, or to taste
1½ cups cognac
1 cup blanched almonds
1 orange, unpeeled, very thinly sliced
1 lemon, unpeeled, very thinly sliced

In a large covered glass or stainless steel pot (we use our slow-cooker), stir together the red wine, the muscatel wine, the vermouth, the cardamoms, the cloves, and the cinnamon sticks. Add the raisins and the orange peel.

Heat until just under a boil. Turn off the heat, cover, and let stand for at least 12 hours.

Shortly before ready to serve, add the sugar, stir well, bring again to just under a boil, and turn the heat to the lowest possible setting.

Remove the orange peel, cloves, and cinnamon sticks with a slotted spoon. Discard.

Stir in the cognac and the almonds, float the orange and the lemon slices on the top, and serve at once in mugs or punch glasses with small spoons on the side for scooping up the almonds and raisins.

B.Y.O.B. Punch

PREPARATION TIME: 15-20 MINUTES
CHILLING TIME: 2-4 HOURS
YIELD: 12 SERVINGS

½ cup water
⅓ cup sugar, or to taste
6 cinnamon sticks
6 whole cloves
3 cups apple juice, chilled
3 cups orange juice, chilled
¼ cup lemon juice
lemon slices
assorted liquors (vodka, brandy, rum, etc.)

In a small saucepan, combine the water, the sugar, the cinnamon sticks, and the cloves. Bring to a boil, cover, reduce the heat, and simmer for 10 minutes. Remove the syrup from the heat, strain out the spices, and discard them.

Chill for at least 2 hours, then add the apple juice, the orange juice, and the lemon juice. Pour the chilled punch into a large serving bowl and float the lemon slices on the top. Let your guests add the liquor of choice to their punch cups.

Café Brûlot

PREPARATION TIME: 5-10 MINUTES
YIELD: 8-10 SERVINGS

⅔ cup brandy
1 cinnamon stick
6 whole cloves
1 3-4-inch piece vanilla bean
3 2-inch strips orange peel
3 2-inch strips lemon peel
10 cubes sugar, soaked in brandy
1 quart very strong, hot coffee
whipped cream

Into a chafing dish set over a low-medium flame, pour the brandy, add the cinnamon stick, the cloves, the vanilla bean, the orange peel, and the lemon peel.

Stir in 9 cubes of the brandy-soaked sugar. Place the remaining sugar cube in a large, long-handled metal spoon and ignite it.

Gently (gingerly) lower the metal spoon onto the surface of the hot brandy in the chafing dish and tip it so the flame from the burning sugar cube is transferred to the brandy in the dish.

As soon as the brandy in the chafing dish is ignited, carefully add the coffee. Serve at once in mugs or punch cups, adding a dollop of whipped cream to the top.

Hot Spiced Cider

PREPARATION TIME: 20-30 MINUTES
YIELD: 8-10 SERVINGS

This drink was very popular with the early settlers in Virginia and other southern colonies and our friends and relatives in those regions say it is still a cool- or cold-weather favorite.

8 cups apple cider
1 cinnamon stick
¼ teaspoon nutmeg, or to taste
¼ teaspoon cloves, or to taste
¼ teaspoon allspice, or to taste
whole cloves
1 small orange
¼ cup lemon juice
1 cup white rum (optional)

Combine the cider and the cinnamon stick in a large stainless steel pot and simmer for 15 minutes. Stir in the nutmeg, the cloves, and the allspice to taste.

Keep on very low heat while you wash and dry the orange and stud it thickly with the cloves.

When ready to serve, slice the studded orange into thin circles and float on the hot cider mix. Stir in the lemon juice and the rum and serve hot in punch glasses or mugs.

Wassail

PREPARATION TIME: 60-75 MINUTES
YIELD: 6-8 SERVINGS

Our English ancestors celebrated many of the special occasions in their lives with mugs or cups of this pungent drink. After trying it ourselves, we think we know why the English are often described as having stiff upper lips.

4 cups apple juice
½ cup cranberry juice
⅓ cup molasses
½ teaspoon bitters
1 cinnamon stick
1 small orange, studded with whole cloves
½ cup orange juice
½-1 cup dark rum

Combine the apple juice, the cranberry juice, the molasses, the bitters, and the cinnamon stick in a large stainless steel pot. Cover and simmer for about 1 hour.

When ready to serve, cut the studded orange into thin slices and float on the *WASSAIL*. Add the orange juice and the rum and serve hot in punch glasses or mugs.

Partygoer's Punch

PREPARATION TIME: 5-10 MINUTES
YIELD: 4 SERVINGS

¾ cup sugar, or to taste
1 cup warm water
2 cups light or dark rum
juice of 4 limes
1 cup orange juice
crushed ice
4 orange slices
fresh mint sprigs

In a large pitcher, combine the sugar and the water and stir until the sugar is completely dissolved. Stir in the rum, the lime juice, and the orange juice.

Serve in tall glasses over crushed ice. Garnish each glass with an orange slice and a mint sprig.

Lemonberry Punch

PREPARATION TIME: 10-15 MINUTES
CHILLING TIME: AT LEAST 2 HOURS
YIELD: 6-8 SERVINGS

2 cups raspberries
¾ cup sugar, or to taste
½ cup very strong black tea
juice of 2 lemons
2 cups ginger ale
crushed ice
4 orange wheels (see page 132)

Chill tall glasses in the freezer.

Combine the raspberries and the sugar in a blender and puree. Turn this combination into a large pitcher or mixing bowl and stir in the tea and the lemon juice. Cover and chill for at least 2 hours.

When ready to serve, remove from the refrigerator and add the ginger ale.

Pour the mixture over crushed ice in the chilled glasses. Garnish with an orange wheel on each rim and serve.

Sonnenobst Shake

PREPARATION TIME: 5–10 MINUTES
YIELD: 4 SERVINGS

You can use any citrus juice in this recipe, but we have found that orange, mandarin, tangerine or lemon juice is best.

3 cups milk
½ cup citrus juice
½ cup sugar, or to taste
4 scoops vanilla ice cream
fruit wedges (see page 130)

Combine the milk, the citrus juice, and the sugar in a blender and mix until the sugar is completely dissolved.

Add the ice cream and blend thoroughly.

Pour the mixture into tall glasses, garnish each with a narrow fruit wedge, and serve.

Boston Commons Punch

PREPARATION TIME: 10–15 MINUTES
STANDING TIME: OVERNIGHT
YIELD: 16–20 SERVINGS

The ancestors who settled New England a few hundred years ago were stern, God-fearing folk who worked hard, played hard, and fought hard. Apparently, they also partied hard, if this beverage named after one of their favorite gathering places is any indication. We agree that it deserves the title "Punch," but we don't think it's common.

2 cups boiling water
3 teaspoons tea leaves or 2 tea bags
2 cups sugar, or to taste
juice of 6 lemons
juice of 6 oranges
1 cup brandy
2 cups claret
1 ice ring
1 bottle sparkling dry white wine
orange slices
lemon slices

The day before you plan to serve the *PUNCH,* make a strong tea by pouring the boiling water over the tea leaves or tea bags and let steep for 10 minutes. Strain the tea leaves or remove the tea bags, stir in the sugar until completely dissolved, and cool the liquid.

Add the lemon juice, the orange juice, the brandy, and the claret to the tea. Chill overnight.

Fill an 8-inch ring mold nearly full of water and freeze.

When ready to serve, unmold the ice ring into a large bowl and add the reserved tea mixture.

Add the sparkling wine, float the orange slices and the lemon slices on the top, and serve.

Orange Bounce

1 cup cream sherry
⅓ cup honey
2 cups orange juice
crushed ice
4 orange peel twists (see page 137)

Combine the sherry, the honey, and the orange juice and mix well.

Pour the sherry mixture over crushed ice in tall glasses, garnish each with an orange peel twist, and serve.

Sunday Punch

ice mold
2 cups boiling water
4 teaspoons tea leaves or 3 tea bags
1 cup sugar, or to taste
2 cups orange juice
2 cups pineapple juice
2 cups grapefruit juice
2 cups apricot juice
4 cups ginger ale
orange slices
lemon slices

The day before you plan to serve the *PUNCH,* make an ice mold for the punch bowl by freezing water in a mold, like a heart-shaped baking pan or similar container.

Make the tea by pouring the boiling water over the tea leaves or tea bags. Steep for 10 minutes. Strain the leaves or remove the tea bags. Stir in the sugar until completely dissolved. Set aside to cool.

When ready to serve, unmold the ice into a large bowl, and add the tea and the fruit juices. Stir well.

Add the ginger ale at the last minute, float the orange and the lemon slices on top, and serve.

Tangerine Crush

2 tangerines, peeled, sectioned, and trimmed
2 kiwifruit, peeled and sliced
2 bananas, peeled and sliced
1 cup orange juice
crushed ice
fresh mint sprigs

Chill four tall glasses in the freezer.

Combine the tangerine sections, the kiwifruit, the bananas, and the orange juice in a blender and puree.

Fill the chilled glasses with crushed ice and add the fruit mixture. Garnish each drink with a mint sprig and serve.

Thousand Lakes Fizz

We often include a thermos of this drink in the picnic basket when we take guests on tours around Thousand Lakes Mountain, whose peaks tower over our home in the high desert of the Southwest. The FIZZ is not only delicious and refreshing, it also helps to take one's mind off switchback roads, steep cliffs, and flash floods.

2½ cups milk
4 ounces vodka
8 teaspoons lemon juice
6 teaspoons powdered sugar, or to taste
crushed ice
4 orange peel twists (see page 137)

Combine the milk, the vodka, the lemon juice, and the powdered sugar and blend thoroughly. Fill glasses with crushed ice and add the mixture.

Garnish each glass with an orange peel twist and serve.

Citrus Soda

¾ cup diced orange sections
¾ cup pineapple chunks
2 cups grapefruit juice
½ cup pineapple juice
sugar to taste
4 scoops orange sherbet

Remove the membrane from the orange sections and divide the sections equally with the pineapple chunks in four tall glasses.

Combine the grapefruit juice, the pineapple juice, and the sugar and mix well. Pour equally over the fruit in each glass. Top with a scoop of orange sherbet and serve.

Orange and Egg Nog

PREPARATION TIME: 5-10 MINUTES
YIELD: 4 SERVINGS

The origins of the word nog are unknown, according to Webster's Dictionary, but it means — among other things — a wooden peg, a strong ale, and an alcoholic drink containing beaten eggs and milk. Alcohol is optional in this recipe, to suite your taste.

3 cups orange juice
⅓ cup dry milk powder
¼ cup honey
4 eggs
4 jiggers whiskey (optional)
nutmeg

Combine all the ingredients and beat or blend until perfectly smooth.

Serve the nog in mugs, with a dusting of nutmeg.

Old-Fashioned Lemonade

PREPARATION TIME: 5-10 MINUTES
YIELD: 1 QUART

½ cup sugar, or to taste
3¼ cups warm water
½ cup lemon juice
ice cubes or crushed ice

Stir the sugar into the water until completely dissolved. Add the lemon juice and mix well.

Serve over ice cubes or crushed ice, or cover the lemonade and chill until ready to serve.

Tangerorange Milk Shake

PREPARATION TIME: 5-10 MINUTES
YIELD: 4 SERVINGS

2 oranges, peeled, sectioned, and trimmed
2 tangerines, peeled, sectioned, and trimmed
1½ cups cold milk
8 teaspoons brown sugar
4 maraschino cherries with stems

Put the orange sections, the tangerine sections, the cold milk, and the brown sugar in a blender and puree until frothy.

Pour the shake into four tall glasses. Top each with a bright red maraschino cherry and serve.

"Champagne"

PREPARATION TIME: 15-20 MINUTES
YIELD: 8 SERVINGS

We have put the title of this recipe in quotes for a reason: Champagne is a white sparkling wine made in the province of Champagne in France. The beverage that follows is not white, it is not wine, and it was not made in the province of Champagne in France. Now you know.

1 bottle (1 pint, 12 ounces) ginger ale, chilled
½ cup sugar, or to taste
1 cup water
1 cup grapefruit juice
½ cup orange juice
¼ cup grenadine syrup
lemon peel

Several hours before you plan to serve the "champagne," chill the ginger ale. Frost eight champagne flutes in the freezer.

In a small saucepan, combine the sugar and the water and simmer, stirring constantly, until the sugar is completely dissolved. Remove from the heat and cool the syrup.

In a large mixing bowl or pitcher, stir together the syrup, the grapefruit juice, the orange juice, and the grenadine.

At the last minute, add the chilled ginger ale to the mixture and pour the "champagne" into the frosted flutes. Rub a strip of lemon peel around the rim of each glass and serve.

Orange Mist

PREPARATION TIME: 5-10 MINUTES
YIELD: 10-12 SERVINGS

3 cups orange juice, chilled
1 bottle (750 ml) white champagne, chilled

Several hours ahead of time, chill the orange juice and the champagne. Frost your champagne glasses in the freezer.

At serving time, remove the champagne glasses from the freezer and pour each glass one-third full of chilled orange juice.

Decant the chilled champagne carefully over the orange juice and serve.

Mulled Wine

PREPARATION TIME: 15-20 MINUTES
YIELD: 10-12 CUPS

1 cup water
1 cup sugar, or to taste
6 whole cloves
2 cinnamon sticks
½ teaspoon nutmeg
8 cups burgundy wine
½ cup brandy
juice of ½ lemon
juice of 1 orange
1 whole orange, thinly sliced

Combine the water, the sugar, the cloves, the cinnamon sticks, and the nutmeg in a large saucepan. Bring to a boil, reduce the heat, and simmer for 10 minutes.

Stir in the wine, the brandy, the lemon juice, and the orange juice. Reheat the mixture over low heat. Do not allow to boil.

Serve warm in mugs or punch glasses garnished with the orange slices.

Side Lines Soda

PREPARATION TIME: 10-15 MINUTES
CHILLING TIME: AT LEAST 2 HOURS
YIELD: 14-18 SERVINGS

This drink goes down very well while watching and cheering on your favorite tennis, golf or baseball stars. It can be put together the day before, except for the club soda, which should be added when served.

1 6-ounce can frozen concentrated limeade, undiluted
4 cups apple cider
4 cups cranberry juice
4 cups club soda
crushed ice
1 lime, thinly sliced

Combine the limeade concentrate, the cider, and the cranberry juice in a large glass or stainless steel container and blend well.

Chill the mixture covered for at least 2 hours.

When ready to serve, remove from the refrigerator, stir in the club soda, and pour over crushed ice in tall glasses. Garnish each drink with a lime slice.

Provincetown Pick-Me-Up

PREPARATION TIME: 15–20 MINUTES
STANDING TIME: 1 MONTH
YIELD: ABOUT 7 CUPS

The hardy folk who debarked from the Mayflower in 1620 had no idea of the trials, troubles, and tribulations that awaited them in the land they were to dub New England. But, to help them when they were down they brought recipes from Old England for some really substantial pick-me-ups like this one. It keeps as long as it can be hidden from the nippers and is good before dinner, after a meal or by the tablespoon in a cup of hot tea. Since it takes a long time to steep, we stagger the times when we start it so that when one batch is nearly gone, another batch is nearly ready.

2 lemons
4 cups brandy
1 teaspoon nutmeg
½ fifth light rum
1 cup sugar

Wash and have ready a large glass container such as an empty wine bottle with a good lid or a tight-fitting cork.

Cut as many thin strips of peeling from the lemons as possible. Be careful not to cut through to the albedo, or white pith under the skins of the fruits. Put the strips of peel into the bottle.

Roll the lemons until soft (see page 128), cut them in half crosswise, and squeeze out all the juice. Pour the juice into the bottle over the peel.

Add the brandy and the nutmeg to the lemon juice and peel. Put the lid on the bottle (or replace the cork) and put the bottle into the refrigerator. Let stand for 2 weeks.

At the end of the 2 weeks, add the rum and stir in the sugar until completely dissolved. Put the bottle back into the refrigerator and let steep for another 2 weeks.

At the end of that time, pour the liquid through a strainer into another container. Ladle the strained *PICK-ME-UP* into small bottles, jars or decanters with lids and store in the refrigerator. Serve when needed.

Hot Toddy

We haven't had a ruling from the Food and Drug Administration on the subject, but around our house toddies are medicinal. We know from years of experience that — properly applied — they definitely make cold and flu sufferers feel better. Should you be immune to such ailments, you still should mix up some of this toddy just for the taste of it.

2 cups water
½ cup honey, or to taste
¼ cup lemon juice
½ cup Scotch whiskey

Combine the water and the honey in a small saucepan and bring to a boil, stirring until the honey is completely dissolved.

Remove the pan from the heat and stir in the lemon juice and the whiskey. Serve at once in a mug or cup.

Omelette Orange

PREPARATION TIME: 15 MINUTES
YIELD: 2 SERVINGS

This is an elegant breakfast or late-night supper dish. Amounts can be increased to accommodate more than two portions. We serve the omelette with toasted and buttered cinnamon bread and flutes of ORANGE MIST (see page 29).

1 orange
1 tablespoon butter or margarine
2 tablespoons honey
1 tablespoon milk
4 eggs
salt to taste
1 teaspoon minced parsley

Peel and section the orange. Remove all of the membrane and cut the sections into bite-sized pieces. Set aside.

Heat the butter or margarine in a special omelette or heavy frying pan until bubbling but not smoking.

Whisk the honey, the milk, the eggs, and the salt together.

When the pan is hot enough, turn the egg mixture into the pan. Lower the heat and cook until the edges begin to crisp and turn brown and the top is somewhat firm.

With a spatula or pancake turner lightly score the omelette across the center, dividing it into two half-circles. Arrange the reserved orange pieces on one of the half-circles. Carefully lift the outer edge of the other half of the omelette with the spatula and fold it over the orange pieces.

Turn off the heat and let the omelette continue to cook with the heat remaining in the pan. When done to your liking, dust with the parsley.

Slide the omelette from the pan and onto a serving platter, or cut it into portions and serve on individual plates.

Instant Breakfast

PREPARATION TIME: 5-10 MINUTES
YIELD: 4 SERVINGS

4 eggs
1½ cups orange juice
1½ cups milk
4 tablespoons honey
dash nutmeg

Combine the eggs, the orange juice, the milk, and the honey in a blender and mix well.

Pour into four tall glasses, dust with nutmeg, and serve.

Muesli Our Way

PREPARATION TIME: 15-20 MINUTES
STANDING TIME: AT LEAST 2 HOURS
YIELD: 4-6 SERVINGS

We became addicted to MUESLI in Switzerland a couple of years ago. It's the national dish there and is offered on the menus of most restaurants. It can be a simple sturdy soaked raw oatmeal with fruit or a frothy, elegant affair loaded with whipped cream and calories — depending on personal tastes or on the time of day it's served. Mix or match the optional additions to suit yourself.

1 cup cold water
1 cup quick-cooking raw oatmeal
juice of ½ lemon
4 tablespoons honey
½ cup bite-sized mandarin or tangerine pieces
½ cup heavy cream, whipped
½ cup coarsely chopped nuts
½ cup dried apricots, dates, figs (optional)
¼ cup shredded coconut (optional)
1 unpeeled apple, shredded (optional)
1 cup whipped nondairy topping (optional)
cinnamon and nutmeg

Combine the cold water and the oatmeal and let stand until the oatmeal is soft. (Proper Swiss put old-fashioned oatmeal to soak the night before.) Add a little more water if you think the mixture is too thick.

When ready to serve, stir in the lemon juice, the honey, and the citrus pieces. Spoon the whipped cream onto each serving and sprinkle with the nuts. Set out containers of any of the optional ingredients, along with the cinnamon and the nutmeg.

Cinnamon and Citrus Toast

PREPARATION TIME: 10 MINUTES
YIELD: 4 SERVINGS

8 slices whole wheat bread
grated peel of 1 orange
½ cup sugar
butter or margarine, softened
cinnamon

Preheat the broiler and have the broiler tray ready. Set out the bread.

Combine the orange peel and the sugar and enough butter or margarine to bind them and to cover the slices of bread. Spread this orange mixture onto the bread slices. Sprinkle each slice with the cinnamon.

Place the slices on the broiler tray and position the tray so the bread is at least 5 inches from the heating element. When the topping starts to bubble, remove the bread from the broiler and serve.

Fruit in Batter

PREPARATION TIME: 10-20 MINUTES
YIELD: 4-6 SERVINGS

Fruchte in Backteig is the type of treat one comes to expect for one's breakfast in Austria's fine old hotels. This recipe comes very close to being as good as the dish we were served in Villach a couple of years ago.

vegetable oil
2 eggs
¾ cup milk
2 tablespoons oil
2 tablespoons lemon juice
2 tablespoons brandy
1-1¼ cups flour
pinch of salt
1 tablespoon sugar
1 orange, peeled, sectioned, and trimmed
1 tangerine, peeled, sectioned, and trimmed
1 grapefruit, peeled, sectioned, and trimmed
powdered sugar

Pour approximately one inch of oil in a heavy pot or frying pan and begin to heat.

Beat the eggs, the milk, the oil, the lemon juice, and the brandy together, then add 1 cup of the flour, the salt, and the sugar to make a smooth, fine batter. If it doesn't look thick enough to coat the citrus pieces, use the other ¼ cup of flour.

When the oil is hot, dip the citrus pieces into the batter, and fry to a golden brown on both sides.

Carefully remove the pieces from the hot oil with a slotted spoon or spatula and drain on paper towels.

Dust the crispy fruit sections with the powdered sugar and serve.

Starters

2 pink grapefruit, halved
4 thin slices boiled ham
¼-½ cup pure maple syrup

Preheat the oven to 350°F. Have ready a shallow baking dish large enough for four grapefruit halves.

Loosen the grapefruit sections with a serrated spoon or curved knife. Don't remove them from the shells, but snip out the center pith with kitchen shears.

Cut the ham into narrow strips. Mound the strips on the grapefruit halves and drizzle the syrup equally over them. Arrange the filled halves in the baking dish and place in the oven until heated through, or about 15 minutes.

Remove the grapefruit halves from the oven and serve.

French Toast with Orange Sauce

1 cup brown sugar, packed
1 cup orange juice, divided
2 tablespoons orange zest, divided
oil
3 eggs
½ cup milk
⅛ teaspoon nutmeg
dash of salt
8 slices bread

Make the *ORANGE SAUCE* by combining the brown sugar, ½ cup of the orange juice, and 1 tablespoon of the orange zest in a small saucepan. Cook, stirring constantly, until the mixture has the consistency of a thick syrup. Set the mixture over very low heat to keep warm.

Oil and preheat a heavy frying pan or griddle.

In a large mixing bowl, beat together the eggs, the milk, the other ½ cup of orange juice, the other table-spoon of orange zest, the nutmeg, and the salt until light and frothy.

Dip each slice of bread into the egg mixture and brown lightly on both sides in the frying pan or on the griddle. Serve the toast with the reserved warm *ORANGE SAUCE*.

Toast with a Twist

PREPARATION TIME: 10-15 MINUTES
YIELD: 4-6 SERVINGS

oil
3 eggs
¾ cup milk
2 tablespoons sugar
2 teaspoons lemon zest or lime zest
1 tablespoon lemon juice or lime juice
8 slices cracked wheat bread
butter or margarine
honey or pure maple syrup

Preheat a large oiled frying pan or griddle.

In a large shallow mixing bowl, beat together the eggs, the milk, and the sugar. Add the lemon or lime zest and the lemon or lime juice.

Dip each slice of bread in the egg mixture. Brown lightly on both sides in the preheated oiled frying pan or griddle.

Serve with butter or margarine and warm honey or maple syrup.

Cartwheels Mac Muffin

PREPARATION TIME: 10-15 MINUTES
YIELD: 4 SERVINGS

These are popular with children — in fact, with everyone who is used to meals that can be eaten on the run.

4 slices bacon
1-2 oranges
4 English muffins
butter or margarine
8 thin slices Muenster cheese

Preheat the broiler and have the broiler tray ready.

Cut the bacon slices in two lengthwise and cook until crisp. Drain on paper towels and set aside.

Peel the oranges deeply, removing all the membrane and pith, and cut into thick cartwheels (see page 132). Remove the seeds and center pith. Set the cartwheels aside.

Split the muffins and spread with the butter or margarine. Place a slice of cheese on four of the muffin halves. Add an orange cartwheel, two of the bacon slices, and another slice of cheese.

Place all the muffin halves on the broiler tray and set the tray about 6 inches from the heating element. Broil the plain muffin halves until golden brown on the cut side. Broil the other muffin halves until heated through and the cheese is partially melted.

Remove the muffin halves from the broiler, put the halves together, and serve with the extra orange cartwheels on the side.

waffle batter (see *MINUTE-MIX* page 75)
2 large oranges, peeled and trimmed, sliced
in thick rounds
1 cup pure maple syrup
¾ teaspoon cinnamon
½ cup crushed wheat cereal flakes
¼ cup ground pecans

Preheat the broiler and the waffle iron. Prepare the waffle batter. Arrange the orange rounds on a baking sheet.

In a small saucepan, combine the syrup and the cinnamon and simmer for about 5 minutes.

Brush the orange rounds with a small amount of the cinnamon syrup and sprinkle with the crushed wheat flakes and the pecans. Reserve the remainder of the syrup.

Broil the orange rounds for 2 or 3 minutes or until bubbling hot. Bake the waffles in the preheated iron.

Remove the orange rounds from the baking sheet and place one on each waffle. Pour the remaining warm cinnamon syrup over the waffles and serve.

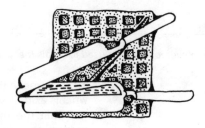

Roquefort Ring-Around

PREPARATION TIME: 15-20 MINUTES
CHILLING TIME: 4 HOURS-OVERNIGHT
YIELD: 1 8-INCH RING MOLD

butter or margarine
1 recipe grapefruit *MADE-FROM-SCRATCH GELATIN* (see page 44)
1 3-ounce package cream cheese, softened
1 teaspoon lime zest
¾ cup crumbled Roquefort cheese
½ cup diced celery
½ cup sour cream
salad greens

Brush the inside of a salad mold lightly with the butter or margarine. Set aside.

Prepare the grapefruit gelatin according to directions on page 44. Turn into a medium mixing bowl and chill.

Blend the cream cheese, the lime zest, and the Roquefort cheese in a small mixing bowl. Set aside.

When the gelatin has set to the consistency of egg whites, blend with the cheese mixture. Fold in the celery and the sour cream.

Turn the gelatin into the mold, cover with plastic wrap or foil, and chill for at least 4 hours — preferably overnight.

When the gelatin is ready, arrange a bed of crisp salad greens on a serving plate. Run a little hot water over the bottom of the mold to loosen it. Unmold the *RING-AROUND* onto the greens, place a mound of crisp greens in the center of the ring, and serve.

Perfect Potato Salad

PREPARATION TIME: 10-15 MINUTES
CHILLING TIME: AT LEAST 4 HOURS
YIELD: 8-10 SERVINGS

We use the adjective perfect *advisedly to describe the best potato salad we've ever had. Like most good things, it is quite simple and straightforward. It can — indeed it should — be made ahead of time so the flavors of the various ingredients blend.*

5 cups cubed cooked potatoes
1 cup coined cooked carrots
dash of black pepper
1 tablespoon sugar
1 teaspoon celery seed
3 tablespoons lemon juice
½ cup finely minced onion
1 cup finely diced celery
1 cup *LEMONNAISE* (see page 45)
½ cup plain low-fat yogurt
4 hard-cooked eggs
salt to taste
1 large carrot, cut into sticks
1 small bunch broccoli, cut into pieces

Turn the potatoes and carrots into a very large mixing bowl and sprinkle with the pepper, the sugar, the celery seed, and the lemon juice. Add the onion and the celery.

In a small mixing bowl, blend the *LEMONNAISE* and the yogurt. Pour this mixture over the potatoes and other ingredients and toss well.

Remove the shells from the eggs, cut the eggs into quarters, and slice the quarters over the potato mixture. Fold the eggs into the salad gently so they retain their identity as eggs, but are well coated with the dressing. Add the salt to taste.

Cover with plastic wrap or foil and chill for at least 4 hours.

Serve on a bed of crisp salad greens and garnish with the carrot sticks and the broccoli pieces.

Avocado Salad Ring

PREPARATION TIME: 10-15 MINUTES
CHILLING TIME: AT LEAST 4 HOURS
YIELD: 1 8-INCH RING MOLD

1 recipe grapefruit *MADE-FROM-SCRATCH GELATIN* (see page 44)
½ cup trimmed grapefruit sections, diced
½ cup trimmed orange sections, diced
2 avocados, peeled, pitted, and cut into bite-sized pieces
salad greens

Prepare the grapefruit gelatin according to directions on page 44.

Place the gelatin, covered, in the refrigerator until it begins to thicken. At that point, stir in the grapefruit sections, the orange sections, and the avocado pieces.

Rinse a ring mold in very cold water and turn the gelatin mixture into the mold. Chill until firm.

Arrange a bed of crisp salad greens on a serving plate. Run a little hot water over the bottom of the mold to loosen it. Unmold the salad onto the greens and serve.

Cool Slaw

PREPARATION TIME: 15-20 MINUTES
CHILLING TIME: 2-4 HOURS
YIELD: 4-6 SERVINGS

⅓ cup sour cream
¼ cup *LEMONNAISE* (see page 45)
1 tablespoon sugar
¼ teaspoon salt, or to taste
⅛ teaspoon black pepper, or to taste
2 tablespoons lemon juice
1 cup mandarin sections
2 cups shredded cabbage
½ cup diced celery
salad greens
nutmeg

In a small mixing bowl, thoroughly blend the sour cream, the *LEMONNAISE*, the sugar, the salt, the pepper, and the lemon juice.

Toss the mandarin sections, the cabbage, and the celery together in a large mixing or salad bowl. Pour the sour cream mixture over the ingredients and fold together carefully.

Cover with foil or plastic wrap and chill for at least 2 hours.

Arrange each portion on a bed of crisp salad greens, sprinkle on a little nutmeg, and serve.

Frozen Fruit Salad

PREPARATION TIME: 10-15 MINUTES
FREEZING TIME: OVERNIGHT
YIELD: 4-6 SERVINGS

1 cup mandarin sections
1 cup pineapple chunks
1 3-ounce package cream cheese, softened
1 cup nondairy whipped topping
½ cup chopped nuts
salad greens

Cut the mandarin sections into bite-sized pieces. Combine the pieces with the pineapple chunks and set aside.

In a medium mixing bowl, beat the cream cheese into the whipped topping and blend well. Fold in the reserved fruits and the chopped nuts.

Pour the mixture into a glass or plastic container, cover with a tight-fitting lid, foil or plastic wrap, and place in the freezer overnight or until frozen solid.

Remove from the freezer 30 minutes before serving to soften slightly. Cut into portions, arrange the portions on crisp salad greens, and serve at once.

Shrimp Salad

1½ cups cooked, deveined small shrimp
½ cup pineapple chunks
1 cup trimmed orange, tangerine or mandarin
    sections, halved
1 cup thinly sliced celery
BASIC SALAD DRESSING (see page 47)
salad greens

In a large mixing bowl, combine the shrimp, the pineapple chunks, the citrus sections, and the celery.

Start with ⅛ cup of the dressing and fold it into the other ingredients. Add more if necessary.

Arrange a bed of crisp salad greens on a platter or in a salad bowl. Turn the shrimp mixture onto the greens and serve.

Salad Nests

2 large oranges
¼ cup diced celery
¼ cup pineapple chunks
¼ cup pecan meats
½ teaspoon nutmeg
LEMONNAISE (see page 45)
shredded lettuce
salad greens

Cut the oranges in half (see page 138). Scoop out the "meat" of the oranges, being careful not to break through the skins. Discard the seeds, the pith, and the membrane. Cut the orange pieces into small bits.

Combine the orange bits in a mixing bowl with the celery, the pineapple, and the pecans.

In a small mixing bowl, blend the nutmeg with the *LEMONNAISE*. Fold this combination through the orange mixture until well coated.

Make a nest of the shredded lettuce in the four orange cups. Spoon the orange mixture into the cups. Place each orange half on a bed of crisp salad greens and serve.

Set Salad

"Set Salad" is what Grandmother Smith called molded gelatin combinations — the "setting" referring to the jelling of the base. This version would ordinarily call for all fresh fruits, but we have found that fresh or frozen pineapple prevents the gelatin from setting, so we have used canned pineapple chunks instead.

1 8-ounce can pineapple chunks
⅛ cup lemon juice
orange juice
1 envelope unflavored gelatin
1 3-ounce package cream cheese, softened
1 mandarin, peeled, sectioned, and trimmed
½ cup diced celery
salad greens

Drain the pineapple. Set aside. Add the lemon juice and enough orange juice to the pineapple liquid to make 2 cups. Pour the liquid into a medium saucepan. Sprinkle the gelatin powder over the combined fruit juices and let stand for 5 minutes.

Slowly heat the mixture to just under a boil, stirring constantly until the gelatin is completely dissolved. Remove from the heat and cool to room temperature.

Blend the cream cheese into the gelatin. Cover the mixture and refrigerate until it has the consistency of egg whites.

Cut the mandarin sections into bite-sized pieces. Combine the pieces, the reserved pineapple, and the celery. Fold into the gelatin.

Chill for at least 4 hours or until firm. Spoon the gelatin mixture onto crisp salad greens and serve.

Our Favorite Tuna Salad

2 cups cooked seashell macaroni
1 cup grated carrots
1 cup mandarin sections
1 cup diced celery
1 green onion, minced
1 9½-ounce can water-packed tuna, drained
1 tablespoon lemon juice
***LEMONNAISE* (see page 45)**
salad greens
1 orange

Combine the cooked macaroni, the carrots, the mandarin sections, the celery, the onion, and the tuna in a large mixing bowl and toss together. Sprinkle the lemon juice over the mixture. Add enough *LEMON-NAISE* to moisten and fold through until well coated.

Cover and chill for at least 2 hours.

Turn the chilled salad onto a bed of crisp salad greens. Cut the orange into paper-thin slices, arrange around the edge for garnish and serve.

Made-From-Scratch Gelatin

PREPARATION TIME: 10-15 MINUTES
CHILLING TIME: 2-4 HOURS
YIELD: 2 CUPS

Making your own flavored gelatin from "scratch" allows you to use fresh fruit juices with all their vitamins and minerals. Such homemade gelatins are much paler than the prepared varieties because they have no artificial coloring. Their taste is much brighter because they have no artificial flavoring. If you want to add anything to the gelatin, such as grated carrots, orange bits or banana chunks, stir them in when it has firmed to the consistency of unbeaten egg whites.

1 envelope unflavored gelatin
2 cups orange, tangerine or grapefruit juice, divided
⅓ cup sugar, or to taste
⅛ teaspoon salt
1 tablespoon lemon juice

Sprinkle the gelatin over ½ cup of the citrus juice in a medium saucepan and stir over low heat until the gelatin is *completely* dissolved. (This is most important because if it isn't completely dissolved, the gelatin will not set properly and will be grainy and unpleasant to the taste.)

Dissolve the sugar and the salt in the gelatin mixture, remove the pan from the heat, and stir in the lemon juice and the remainder of the citrus juice.

Pour into several individual molds or one large mold. Place in the refrigerator to set. When firm, unmold and serve.

Simple Fruit Salad

PREPARATION TIME: 10-15 MINUTES
YIELD: 4-6 SERVINGS

2 tangerines, mandarins or oranges
2 bananas
1 Delicious apple
1 tablespoon lemon juice
½ cup coarsely chopped English walnuts
HONEY AND ORANGE DRESSING (see page 47)
salad greens

Peel, section, and trim the citrus fruits. Cut the sections into bite-sized pieces and put into a large mixing bowl.

Peel the bananas and cut into bite-sized chunks. Wash the apple, cut into quarters, remove the core, and cut the quarters into bite-sized pieces.

Combine the citrus pieces, the banana chunks, and the apple pieces. Sprinkle the lemon juice over the mixture. Add the walnuts and toss well. Fold the salad dressing through the fruits so all are coated.

Turn the mixture onto crisp salad greens and serve.

Lemonnaise

PREPARATION TIME: 10-15 MINUTES
YIELD: ABOUT 1 CUP

1 egg white
½ teaspoon dry mustard
½ teaspoon sugar
⅛ teaspoon salt, or to taste
1 cup safflower or sunflower oil
1½ tablespoons lemon juice
½ tablespoon hot water

Combine the egg white, the mustard, the sugar, and the salt in a deep mixing bowl and beat together until frothy.

Gradually add half the oil, pouring slowly in a thin stream with the mixer running. Slowly add 1 tablespoon of the lemon juice, mixing constantly.

With the mixer running, dribble in the remaining half of the oil and the remaining half-tablespoon of the lemon juice. Add the hot water and continue to mix until thoroughly blended and the mixture has the color and consistency of prepared mayonnaise.

The *LEMONNAISE* may be used at once or stored in a covered glass or plastic container in the refrigerator. It will keep just like commercial mayonnaise.

Orange Dressing

PREPARATION TIME: 15-20 MINUTES
YIELD: ABOUT 1 CUP

This delicious dressing has more than just its taste to recommend it: One serving has only about 30 calories.

3 tablespoons vegetable oil
1 teaspoon sugar
⅛ teaspoon salt, or to taste
½ teaspoon dry mustard
⅛ teaspoon paprika
1 cup orange juice, divided
2 teaspoons cornstarch

Mix the oil, the sugar, the salt, the mustard, and the paprika together in a medium mixing bowl. Set aside.

Put ½ cup of the orange juice into a small saucepan. Stir in the cornstarch and cook over low heat, stirring constantly, until the mixture comes to a boil and thickens. Remove from the heat.

Turn the cornstarch mixture into the reserved oil mixture and beat together until smooth. Blend in the remaining orange juice.

Pour into a covered glass or plastic container and store in the refrigerator until ready to use.

Curried Citrus Dressing

Mrs. Moore, a friend of the family for many years, brought the basic recipe for this dressing from India. It has always been one of our favorites.

1 egg yolk
4 teaspoons lemon or lime juice
½ teaspoon lemon or lime zest
½ cup *LEMONNAISE* (see page 45)
½ cup plain low-fat yogurt
curry powder to taste

Beat the egg yolk in a small saucepan until lemon-colored. Blend in the lemon or lime juice and the lemon or lime zest. Cook the mixture over low heat, stirring constantly, until thick.

Remove from the heat and cool to room temperature.

Blend in the *LEMONNAISE* and the yogurt. Add the curry powder to taste, starting with the tiniest of pinches. Check the seasonings and add more curry powder if necessary.

If the dressing is not to be used at once, store in the refrigerator in a covered glass or plastic container. Bring to room temperature before serving.

Fresh Fruit Dressing

This dressing enhances the flavors of fresh fruits and also adds an unusual touch to salads made with canned or dried fruit.

2 tablespoons lemon juice
2 tablespoons lime juice
⅔ cup peanut or other mild vegetable oil
½ teaspoon lemon zest
½ teaspoon lime zest
⅓ cup sugar
½ teaspoon dry mustard
1 tablespoon caraway seeds

Combine the lemon juice and the lime juice with the oil in a blender or covered jar and blend or shake until thoroughly mixed with a cloudy or milky look.

Add the lemon zest, the lime zest, the sugar, and the mustard and mix or blend together thoroughly. Stir in the caraway seeds.

If the dressing is not to be used at once, store in the refrigerator in a covered glass or plastic container. Bring to room temperature before serving.

Basic Salad Dressing

½ cup lemon juice
1 tablespoon sugar
¼ teaspoon salt, or to taste
¼ teaspoon pepper
1½ cups vegetable oil

Combine all the ingredients in a blender or a jar with a tight lid. Blend or shake the ingredients together until creamy and frothy.

If the dressing is not to be used at once, store in a covered glass or plastic container in the refrigerator. Bring to room temperature before serving.

Honey and Orange Dressing

¼ cup frozen concentrated orange juice, undiluted
¼ cup honey
1 tablespoon lemon juice
½ teaspoon dry mustard
⅛ teaspoon salt, or to taste
⅔ cup peanut oil

Combine the orange juice concentrate, the honey, the lemon juice, the mustard, and the salt in a blender or deep mixing bowl. Blend together or beat with an electric mixer until smooth.

Dribble all the oil very slowly into the other ingredients, beating or blending constantly until the mixture is cloudy and light.

If the dressing is not to be used at once, store in a covered glass or plastic container in the refrigerator.

Boiled Dressing

½ cup dark brown sugar, packed
1 tablespoon flour
1 egg, beaten
¾ cup pineapple juice
3 tablespoons lemon juice
½ cup orange juice

Combine the brown sugar, the flour, the egg, and the pineapple juice in a medium saucepan and cook over low heat, stirring constantly, until thick and smooth.

Remove from the heat and stir in the lemon juice and the orange juice. Allow the dressing to cool to room temperature. Pour into a covered glass or plastic container and chill before using.

Jelled Dressing

PREPARATION TIME: 10-15 MINUTES
YIELD: ABOUT 1 CUP

Make this dressing ahead of time and store, covered, in the refrigerator. When ready to use, remove from the refrigerator and set the dressing in a pan of hot water or pop into the microwave for a few minutes to soften the gelatin so the dressing pours easily. Don't overdo the warm-up. The dressing should be cool when served.

1 envelope unflavored gelatin
½ cup water
2 tablespoons honey
¼ teaspoon soy sauce
⅛ teaspoon dry mustard
⅛ teaspoon garlic powder
2 teaspoons lemon zest
¼ cup lemon juice
1 cup orange juice
salt and pepper to taste

Sprinkle the gelatin over the water in a small saucepan, then stir over low heat until completely dissolved.

Remove from the heat. Blend in the honey, the soy sauce, the mustard, and the garlic powder. Add the lemon zest, the lemon juice, and the orange juice. Check the seasonings. Add the salt and pepper to taste. Store in a covered glass or plastic container in the refrigerator.

Guacamole Dressing

PREPARATION TIME: 10-15 MINUTES
YIELD: ABOUT 1½ CUPS

2 avocados, peeled and pitted
juice of 1 lemon
1-2 tablespoons sugar
¼ cup plain low-fat yogurt
1 tablespoon tomato catsup
1 teaspoon finely minced onion
salt to taste

Combine all the ingredients (start with 1 tablespoon of the sugar and add the other tablespoon if necessary) in a blender or processor and process until smooth and creamy.

If the dressing is not to be used at once, store in a covered glass or plastic container in the refrigerator.

More-Than-Tuna Casserole

PREPARATION TIME: 15–20 MINUTES
BAKING TIME: 45 MINUTES
YIELD: 4–6 SERVINGS

1 lemon
2 tablespoons butter or margarine
1 green onion, minced
2 tablespoons all-purpose flour
2 cups milk
1 9¼-ounce can water-packed tuna
2 cups cooked elbow macaroni
1 cup cooked carrot coins
1 cup cooked broccoli pieces
salt and pepper to taste
½ cup shredded cheese

Preheat the oven to 375°F. Butter a 2-quart covered casserole dish.

Cut the lemon into two halves and remove the seeds. Cut one of the halves into very thin slices and set aside. Chop or grind the other half as fine as possible and set aside.

Heat the butter or margarine in a medium saucepan. Sauté the onion until limp, remove the onion and set aside.

Sprinkle the flour into the remaining butter or margarine and cook until the flour mixture begins to bubble. Add the milk, beating to prevent lumps. Cook the sauce until smooth and thick, stirring constantly. Remove from the heat.

Drain the tuna and toss together with the macaroni, the carrots, the broccoli, the reserved ground-up lemon, and the reserved onion. Fold this combination into the milk sauce and season to taste with the salt and pepper.

Turn the mixture into the casserole dish. Sprinkle with the shredded cheese.

Bake, covered, for 30 minutes, or until the cheese is melted and bubbling. Remove the cover and continue to bake for 15 minutes. Remove from the oven and serve, garnished with the reserved lemon slices.

Chicken and Citrus Sandwich

PREPARATION TIME: 15 MINUTES
YIELD: 4 SERVINGS

¼ cup *LEMONNAISE* (see page 45)
¼ cup plain low-fat yogurt
1 teaspoon prepared mustard
1 cup diced cooked chicken
½ cup diced celery
¼ cup minced onion
2 oranges, peeled, all pith removed
4 pita bread rounds, opened to form pockets
shredded lettuce
alfalfa sprouts

Combine the *LEMONNAISE,* the yogurt, and the mustard into a smooth spread and fold in the chicken, the celery, and the onion, mixing well.

Slice the oranges into eight cartwheels. Tuck two of the orange cartwheels into each of the pita pockets and sandwich one-fourth of the chicken mixture between the two cartwheels.

Sprinkle the opening of each sandwich with the shredded lettuce and the alfalfa sprouts and serve.

Chicken Mac Orange

PREPARATION TIME: 45–60 MINUTES
YIELD: 4 SERVINGS

You won't find this entrée offered at your local take-out restaurant, but it definitely qualifies as fast food. You can prepare it in the broiler section of your oven or on a charcoal grill outside.

1 orange
1 tablespoon Worcestershire sauce
½ teaspoon ginger
salt and pepper to taste
2 small fryer chickens, halved

Preheat the broiler and have the broiler tray ready or bring the charcoal in your grill to the white-ash stage.

Peel the orange and remove all the white membrane and seeds. Grind or chop the pulp and combine with the Worcestershire sauce, the ginger, and the salt and pepper.

Remove all the skin and fat from the chicken pieces. Arrange the pieces on the broiler tray or on the grill, and brown on both sides. Baste each side with the orange mixture, repeating the process until all the sauce is used when the pieces are done.

Serve the chicken with *PERFECT POTATO SALAD* (see page 40).

Steak à la Suisse

Individual fruits may vary in their sweetness, with one grapefruit being mild and delicate in flavor, and another tart and bitter. The amount of brown sugar you use in this recipe will depend on the sweetness of the grapefruit sections and your own taste preferences.

2 tablespoons vegetable oil
1 onion, sliced
1 pound round steak
flour
1 cup dry red wine
1 tablespoon Worcestershire sauce
¼ teaspoon rosemary
¼ teaspoon thyme
¼ teaspoon basil
water
1 grapefruit, peeled, sectioned, and trimmed
2 large carrots, quartered
brown sugar to taste
salt and pepper to taste

Heat the oil in a heavy covered pan and sauté the onion slices until translucent. Remove the onion slices and set aside.

Trim off all fat from the meat. Dredge the meat in enough flour to coat well. Pound the flour into the meat with a table knife or a steak pounder to take up as much flour as possible. Cut the meat into serving pieces.

Sauté the meat over medium-high heat in the remaining oil, letting it get quite brown on both sides. Turn the heat to simmer and gradually stir in the wine, the Worcestershire sauce, the rosemary, the thyme, and the basil, and enough water to make a smooth, light gravy.

Stir in the grapefruit sections and the carrots, cover, and cook over low heat for 15 minutes. Check the sauce, add the brown sugar, and the salt and pepper to taste.

Continue to simmer the steak for at least 1 hour or until very tender. Serve.

Saucy Baked Chicken

PREPARATION TIME: 20–25 MINUTES
BAKING TIME: 45–60 MINUTES
YIELD: 4 SERVINGS

2 tablespoons vegetable oil
¼ cup minced onion
1 small clove garlic, minced
2 chicken breasts, halved
½ lemon, thinly sliced
salt and pepper to taste
dash paprika
¼ cup minced parsley
¼ cup lemon juice
1 cup plain low-fat yogurt
parsley sprigs

Preheat the oven to 375°F. Have ready a covered baking dish.

Heat the oil in a medium frying pan and sauté the onion and the garlic until soft. Remove the onion mixture and set aside.

Remove the skin and fat from the chicken pieces. Brown in the heated oil and place in the baking dish, rib side down.

Arrange the lemon slices and the reserved onion mixture on top of the chicken pieces. Sprinkle with the salt and pepper, the paprika, and the parsley.

Bake, covered, for 45–60 minutes or until tender. Remove from the casserole and keep warm on a serving dish in the oven.

Stir the lemon juice and the yogurt into the drippings and liquid remaining in the casserole and heat the sauce to just under a boil, stirring constantly.

Spoon the sauce over the reserved chicken pieces and serve, garnished with the parsley sprigs.

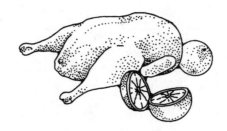

Turkey Delight

No matter how we plan, every time we have turkey — even in the easy-to-manage small portions that are available now in supermarkets — we end up with too much for one meal. However, we haven't complained about having to eat leftovers since we developed this main dish salad. In fact, we've started buying too much turkey on purpose!

¼ cup *LEMONNAISE* (see page 45)
¼ cup plain low-fat yogurt
curry powder to taste
1½ cups tangelo sections, cut into bite-sized
   pieces
1 cup diced melon (any variety)
1½ cups diced cooked turkey
½ cup diced celery
½ cup coarsely chopped walnuts
salad greens

In a large mixing bowl, thoroughly blend the *LEMONNAISE* and the yogurt. Add the curry powder to taste — a pinch at a time. Fold in the tangelo sections, the melon, the turkey, the celery, and the walnuts.

Turn the mixture onto crisp salad greens and serve.

Arizona Meatloaf

3 slices wheat bread, broken into pieces
2 teaspoons lemon zest
2 tablespoons lemon juice
1 cup plain low-fat yogurt
1 egg
1 pound lean ground beef
¼ cup finely chopped onion
½ teaspoon powdered sage
⅛ teaspoon garlic powder
½ teaspoon dry mustard
salt and pepper to taste
1 cup boiling water
parsley sprigs

Preheat the oven to 375°F, and have ready a shallow baking pan at least 8 inches square.

Combine the bread pieces, the lemon zest, the lemon juice, and the yogurt in a large mixing bowl. Beat in the egg and let the mixture stand for a few minutes to soften the bread.

Beat the egg mixture until smooth. Add the ground beef, the onion, the sage, the garlic powder, the mustard, and the salt and pepper to taste. Mix well. Don't be squeamish, use your hands.

Form the meat mixture into a round or oblong loaf. Place in the baking pan and pour the cup of boiling water around the loaf but not over it.

Bake for 45-60 minutes or until well-done. Pour off any fat, slide the loaf onto a serving platter, and garnish with the parsley sprigs.

Sweet and Citrus Tenderloin Tips

PREPARATION TIME: 75–90 MINUTES
YIELD: 4–6 SERVINGS

Aside from its good taste, this main dish has other virtues. It can be made days ahead of time, refrigerated, and reheated just before serving, and it can be stretched to serve extra people, in case unexpected company drops by.

1 pound beef tenderloin
¼ cup all-purpose flour
salt and pepper to taste
¼ teaspoon powdered sage
¼ cup minced parsley
4 tablespoons vegetable oil
½ cup diced onion
2 cups beef broth
1 tablespoon Worcestershire sauce
¼ cup honey
4 lemon slices
4 lime slices

Trim off all the fat from the tenderloin and cut the meat into 2-inch chunks.

Combine the flour, the salt and pepper, the sage, and the parsley in a paper or plastic bag. Add the tenderloin chunks and shake until thoroughly coated. Set the chunks aside.

Heat the oil in a heavy covered saucepan or frying pan and sauté the onion until limp. Remove the onion and set aside while you brown the reserved floured tenderloin chunks on both sides in the heated oil.

Slowly pour the beef broth into the pan, stirring the mixture constantly to prevent lumps. Add the Worcestershire sauce and the honey. Bring to a boil, then reduce to simmer.

Remove the rind from the lemon and the lime slices and cut each slice into quarters. Stir the quarters into the beef mixture. Cover the pan and cook over low heat for at least 60 minutes, or until the meat is fork-tender. Serve.

Jambon au Vin Blanc

1 4-5 pound precooked boneless ham
1 ½ cups dry white wine
1 cup apple juice or cider
6 whole cloves
½ cup finely chopped leeks
1 lemon
¼ cup butter or margarine
3 tablespoons all-purpose flour
½-1 cup chicken broth
¼ cup lemon juice
¼ cup brown sugar, packed

Trim off as much fat as possible from the ham and place cut side down in a deep covered pan. Combine the wine and the juice or cider and pour over the meat. Add the cloves and the leeks.

Bring the liquids to a boil, reduce to simmer, cover, and cook until the ham is meltingly tender — at least 1½ hours. Remove from the pan and keep warm. Strain the pan juices and set aside.

Cut the lemon into thin slices and set aside.

Melt the butter or margarine in a medium sauce-pan and stir in the flour, making a smooth paste. Add the reserved pan juices, ½ cup of the chicken broth, the lemon juice, and the brown sugar. Whisk until smooth, adding more broth if too thick.

Remove from the heat and pour into a gravy boat or sauce pitcher.

Carve the ham into thin slices and arrange on a serving platter. Garnish with the lemon slices and serve.

Boeuf en Marinade

PREPARATION TIME: 15-20 MINUTES
COOKING TIME: 1-3 HOURS

MARINATING TIME: AT LEAST 12 HOURS
YIELD: 8-10 SERVINGS

4-pound sirloin tip roast
2 cloves garlic
1 bay leaf
1 onion
1 carrot
6 peppercorns
1 teaspoon sage leaves
salt to taste
1 orange
½–1 cup orange juice
¼–½ cup pan juices/beef broth
¼ cup dry red wine
parsley sprigs

Place a heavy, covered pan over high heat until a few drops of water dance on the surface. Sear the beef on all sides to seal in the juices.

Turn the heat to low, add the garlic, the bay leaf, the onion, the carrot, the peppercorns, the sage, and the salt to taste. Cover and cook the beef until fork-tender.

If necessary, add a little beef broth to keep the beef from burning. When the beef is done, remove from the pan and let cool completely.

Strain the pan juices and set aside. Cut the cooled beef into thin slices and arrange on a serving dish or platter.

Cut the orange into paper-thin slices. Arrange the orange slices on top of the sliced beef.

Combine ½ cup of the orange juice, ¼ cup of the reserved pan juices, and the wine. Pour this mixture over the beef. Increase the amounts of orange juice and pan juices or beef broth if necessary to have enough marinade to cover the beef. Cover with plastic wrap or foil and chill for at least 12 hours.

When ready to serve, garnish the platter with the parsley sprigs.

Salmon Mousse

1 15½-ounce can red or pink salmon
water
2 envelopes unflavored gelatin
1 stalk celery, cut into small chunks
1 small onion, quartered
¼ cup parsley
1 cup whipping cream
¾ cup *LEMONNAISE* (see page 45)
¼ cup lemon juice
⅛ teaspoon dill seed
½ teaspoon salt, or to taste
salad greens
2 hard-cooked eggs

Drain the salmon, reserving the liquid. Set the salmon aside.

In a medium saucepan, sprinkle the gelatin over the reserved salmon liquid, adding enough water to make 1 cup. Let stand for 5 minutes, then stir over low heat until the gelatin is completely dissolved, at least 5 minutes.

Combine the gelatin mixture with the celery, the onion, the parsley, the whipping cream, the *LEMONNAISE*, and the lemon juice in a blender or processor. Add the reserved salmon, the dill seed, and the salt and process until blended.

Turn the mixture into a 6-cup mold or bowl and chill until firm, at least 4 hours.

Unmold onto a bed of crisp salad greens, arrange the hard-cooked eggs, cut into thin slices around the *MOUSSE*, and serve.

Poached Red Snapper

We have found that fish poached in this simple way is simply delicious. It can be prepared ahead of time and warmed up before serving, with no loss of flavor or tenderness.

2 tablespoons butter or margarine
4 boneless red snapper fillets
1 small lemon, sliced
¾ teaspoon lime zest
¼ cup minced onion
2 tablespoons minced parsley
salt and pepper to taste

Melt the butter or margarine in a large covered frying pan. Arrange the snapper fillets one layer deep in the pan. Place a lemon slice on each fillet, along with a pinch of the lime zest.

Sprinkle the onion and the parsley over the fillets, cover, and simmer for 10-15 minutes, or until the fish flakes when tested with a fork. Add the salt and pepper to taste.

Remove the fish fillets to a serving platter and keep warm.

Strain the pan juices, pour into a small pitcher or gravy boat on the side, and serve with the fillets.

Ensalada de Pollo con Queso

2 grapefruit
2 cups cubed cooked chicken
¼ cup finely chopped celery
1 green onion, minced
¼ cup *LEMONNAISE* (see page 45)
¼ cup plain low-fat yogurt
salt and pepper to taste
1 cup shredded low-fat mozzarella cheese
salad greens
minced parsley

Cut the grapefruit in half. Working over a large mixing bowl so that none of the juice is lost, cut around the sections with a serrated grapefruit knife or spoon, lift the sections from the shells, remove membrane and seeds, and cut into bite-sized pieces. Add the chicken, the celery, and the onion to the grapefruit pieces. Set aside.

Scoop out and discard membrane and pith from the grapefruit shells. Set the shells aside.

In a small mixing bowl, blend the *LEMONNAISE* and the yogurt with the salt and pepper. Pour over the grapefruit mixture in the large bowl and toss together until coated.

Spoon part of the grapefruit mixture into the reserved grapefruit shells. Mound generously and top each with ⅛ cup of the cheese.

Arrange a bed of crisp salad greens in a separate serving dish and turn the remainder of the grapefruit mixture onto it so that second helpings are available. Sprinkle the rest of the cheese over the top.

Dust each salad with minced parsley and serve.

Lemon-Fried Chicken

PREPARATION TIME: 45-60 MINUTES
YIELD: 4-6 SERVINGS

Chicken prepared this way is equally good served hot at a sit-down meal or cold at a picnic. For variation, substitute orange peel for lemon.

2 tablespoons grated lemon peel
½ cup grated Parmesan cheese
½ cup dry bread crumbs
1 teaspoon powdered sage
½ teaspoon oregano
salt and pepper to taste
4 tablespoons butter or margarine
4 chicken breasts, halved

In a small bowl, stir together the lemon peel, the cheese, the bread crumbs, the sage, the oregano, and the salt and pepper to taste. Set aside.

Put a large frying pan over low heat and melt the butter or margarine. Pour the melted butter or margarine into a small bowl. Increase the heat to medium.

Remove skin and fat from the chicken. Dip the chicken pieces first into the melted butter or margarine, then into the crumb mixture. Arrange the coated chicken pieces in the heated pan and cook until well done and tender, turning once.

Remove the chicken pieces and drain on paper towels. Serve or chill for serving cold later.

Lemon Butter Sauce

PREPARATION TIME: 5-10 MINUTES
YIELD: ½ CUP

Over the years we've experimented with several variations of LEMON BUTTER SAUCE, *most of which have had the same basic ingredients. This is one of our favorites — very good with fish and superb with lobster.*

½ cup butter
juice of 1 lemon
slivered almonds (optional)
chopped chives (optional)

Melt the butter in a small saucepan, add the juice, and bring to just under a boil.

Remove from the heat and whisk until frothy. Serve the sauce while still warm with the slivered almonds or the chives added.

Barbecue Sauce

PREPARATION TIME: 10-15 MINUTES
YIELD: ABOUT 1 CUP

Baste barbecued ribs, grilled hamburgers, hot dogs or roast chicken with this zesty sauce. It can be made ahead of time and stored in the refrigerator until needed.

1 tablespoon butter or margarine
¼ cup minced onion
juice and zest of 1 orange
juice of 1 lemon
1 teaspoon lemon zest
⅓ cup chili sauce or catsup
2 tablespoons molasses
1 tablespoon Worcestershire sauce
salt and pepper to taste

Heat the butter or margarine in small saucepan and sauté the onion until limp and translucent.

Stir in the remaining ingredients and cook over low heat for about 15 minutes.

Remove from the heat and serve or store in the refrigerator in a covered glass or plastic container.

Sweet and Sour Sauce

PREPARATION TIME: 15-20 MINUTES
YIELD: ABOUT 1½ CUPS

This sauce is good as an accompaniment for ham, chicken or pork dishes.

¼ cup dark brown sugar, packed
2 teaspoons cornstarch
½ teaspoon dry mustard
¾ cup tangerine juice
1 tablespoon lemon juice
1 teaspoon Worcestershire sauce
1 teaspoon grated tangerine peel
2 tangerines, peeled, sectioned, and seeded

In a small saucepan, combine the brown sugar, the cornstarch, and the mustard. Gradually stir in the tangerine juice, the lemon juice, the Worcestershire sauce, and the tangerine peel.

Cook over medium heat until thick, stirring constantly. Cut the tangerine sections into bite-sized pieces and fold into the sauce.

Remove from the heat and serve or store in a covered glass or plastic container in the refrigerator.

Lemondaise Sauce

½ cup butter or margarine
⅛ teaspoon paprika
juice of ½ lemon
3 egg yolks

Melt the butter or margarine in the top of a double boiler over hot water, or in a small saucepan set into a larger pan of hot water. Stir in the paprika.

Add the lemon juice drop by drop, beating constantly with a wire whisk or electric mixer. Beat in the egg yolks one at a time in the same manner.

Continue to beat the mixture until light and fluffy, with a slight sheen. Remove from the heat and serve.

PREPARATION TIME: 15 MINUTES
CHILLING TIME: 2 HOURS
YIELD: 4 SERVINGS

Solsken Soppa

Grandmother Westlund used to make a special soup for holidays like Christmas. Her Fruktsoppa featured stewed dried apricots, prunes, raisins, dates, currants, and figs — ingredients that were rather exotic in a cold northern country like Sweden. The liquid from the stewed fruits was thickened with a little tapioca and the dish was served hot. In contrast, SOLSKEN SOPPA (SUNSHINE SOUP) — though still with a Swedish accent — features fruits that are now available fresh year-round, even in Sweden. It requires no cooking and is served cold.

1 large orange
1 tangerine
1 tangor
1 banana
1 peach or 1 cup canned peaches
1 cup pineapple chunks or 1 cup canned
   crushed pineapple
honey or sugar to taste
chopped nuts
nutmeg

Remove the peel, seeds, and pith from the citrus fruits and puree the fruit in a blender or processor. Pour the puree into a large mixing bowl.

Puree the banana, the peach, and the pineapple. Add to the orange mixture. Stir in the honey or sugar to taste until completely dissolved.

Cover and chill for at least 2 hours. Serve with a dish of chopped nuts and a shaker of nutmeg on the side.

Potage au Vin

PREPARATION TIME: 20-25 MINUTES
CHILLING TIME: 4 HOURS (OPTIONAL)
YIELD: 6-8 SERVINGS

2½ cups water
⅛ cup tapioca
2 egg yolks
½ cup sugar, divided
½ cup raisins
½ tablespoon lemon zest
¼ cup lemon juice
¼ cup orange juice
1½ cups cream sherry

Mix the water and the tapioca in a medium saucepan and let stand for 5 minutes.

Whisk the egg yolks with the sugar in a small mixing bowl and set aside.

Add the raisins and the lemon zest to the tapioca mixture and bring to a boil over medium heat, stirring often to prevent lumps. When the raisins have plumped, stir in the egg mixture a little at a time, blending thoroughly. Simmer for 5 minutes, remove from the heat, and blend in the lemon juice, the orange juice, and the sherry. Serve.

You may also chill the soup for 4 hours and serve cold.

Summer Soup

PREPARATION TIME: 15 MINUTES
CHILLING TIME: AT LEAST 4 HOURS
YIELD: 6-8 SERVINGS

This superb soup requires so little effort both you and your soup can come to the table looking cool and collected on even the hottest summer day.

4 cups buttermilk
juice of 1 lemon, strained
3 egg yolks
⅓ cup sugar, or to taste
1 teaspoon vanilla
½ cup heavy cream

Chill the buttermilk, the cream, a large mixing bowl, a rotary beater, a wire whisk, and serving dishes for at least 2 hours.

When everything is properly chilled, whisk the buttermilk in the chilled mixing bowl until frothy and light.

In another mixing bowl, beat together the lemon juice, the egg yolks, the sugar, and the vanilla. Fold the egg mixture into the buttermilk a little at a time.

Cover and chill for at least 4 hours. When the soup is icy cold, whip the chilled cream, ladle the soup into the chilled dishes, and top each serving with a swirl of cream. Serve at once.

Mrs. Moore's Lime Soup

PREPARATION TIME: 1½-2 HOURS
YIELD: 6-8 SERVINGS

This light delicate broth is unique in our experience. It is clear and sharp, tart and tantalizing — a good opener for a multicourse meal.

5 cups clear chicken broth
1 very small clove garlic
3 tablespoons brown sugar
¼ cup minced parsley
⅓ cup lime juice
salt and pepper to taste

Bring the broth to a boil in a medium saucepan. Peel the garlic clove and add to the boiling broth along with the brown sugar and the parsley.

Simmer for 10-15 minutes, remove from the heat, and stir in the lime juice and the salt and pepper to taste.

Let stand for at least 1 hour. Remove the garlic clove.

Reheat the soup and serve, or chill and serve cold.

Orange Carrot Soup

PREPARATION TIME: 20-25 MINUTES
YIELD: 6-8 SERVINGS

2 tablespoons butter or margarine
¼ cup minced onion
⅛ teaspoon minced garlic
3 tablespoons all-purpose flour
4 cups chicken broth
2 cups cooked carrot coins
1 orange, peeled, sectioned, and trimmed
½ cup plain low-fat yogurt
salt and pepper to taste

Heat the butter or margarine in a large saucepan. Sauté the onion and the garlic until soft. Remove the onion mixture from the butter or margarine and set aside.

Stir the flour into the pan and cook, stirring constantly until the mixture bubbles. Add the broth gradually, stirring to prevent lumps. Cook the mixture until it has the consistency of a medium white sauce.

Remove from the heat. Add the carrots, and the orange sections. Puree the combination in a blender or processor.

Return the puree to the saucepan and reheat to just under a boil.

Fold in the yogurt, add the salt and pepper to taste, and serve, or chill and serve cold.

Overnight Soup

PREPARATION TIME: 10-15 MINUTES   CHILLING TIME: OVERNIGHT
STEEPING TIME: 60 MINUTES   YIELD: 6-8 SERVINGS

3 cups raspberries, fresh or frozen (thawed)
⅓ cup honey
1½ tablespoons cornstarch
1½ cups orange juice, divided
1 tablespoon lemon juice
1½ cups plain low-fat yogurt

Combine the raspberries with the honey in a medium mixing bowl and set aside to steep for 1 hour, then drain the berries. Reserve the juice and the berries separately. Set half of the berries aside. Puree the other half of the berries in a blender or processor and add to the reserved raspberry juice.

Pour the puree into a medium saucepan and bring to just under a boil over medium heat. Dissolve the cornstarch in ¼ cup of the orange juice. Stir into the puree slowly to prevent lumps.

Cook the mixture, stirring constantly until it has the consistency of a light white sauce. Remove from the heat and let cool to room temperature. Stir in the reserved berries, the rest of the orange juice, and the lemon juice. Fold in the yogurt.

Chill overnight before serving.

Avocado Soup

PREPARATION TIME: 10-15 MINUTES
CHILLING TIME: 2-4 HOURS
YIELD: 6-8 SERVINGS

This is a very pretty soup indeed. Soft sage green in color, it has a unique flavor and is especially delicious when made with freshly squeezed grapefruit or pummelo juice.

8 ice cubes
1½ cups grapefruit or pummelo juice
⅛ cup lemon juice
2 large (or 3 small) avocados, peeled and pitted
¼ teaspoon nutmeg
¼ teaspoon cinnamon
1 tablespoon sugar, or to taste
salt to taste
mint sprigs

At least four hours before serving, chill soup cups or plates.

In a blender or processor, combine the ice cubes with the grapefruit or pummelo juice, the lemon juice, and the avocados. Blend until smooth.

Add the nutmeg, the cinnamon, the sugar, and the salt to taste, and blend again.

Serve in the chilled soup cups or plates and garnish with the mint sprigs.

Great Aunt Vic's Hot Buttermilk Soup

PREPARATION TIME: 45–60 MINUTES
YIELD: 6-8 SERVINGS

We must confess that we looked askance when we ran across Great Aunt Victoria's recipe for Hot Buttermilk Soup while going through an old trunk in the attic. Hot Buttermilk Soup? Then we tried the recipe and apologized to Great Aunt Vic's memory for having doubted her.

2 cups buttermilk
1 cup whole milk
1 tablespoon tapioca
1 cinnamon stick
½ cup sugar, or to taste
1 tablespoon lemon juice
nutmeg
lemon peel twists

Simmer the buttermilk, the whole milk, the tapioca, and the cinnamon stick in a large saucepan until the tapioca is cooked, stirring occasionally to prevent burning and sticking. (Don't be dismayed when you see the milks curdle and separate. All will come right in the end.)

Remove from the heat and discard the cinnamon stick. Stir in the sugar until completely dissolved and whisk in the lemon juice.

Dust each bowl with nutmeg, garnish with a lemon peel twist, and serve.

P.S. Great Aunt Vic didn't mention it, but this soup is almost as good when it's chilled. Try it both ways.

Sopa de Naranjas

PREPARATION TIME: 30 MINUTES
CHILLING TIME: AT LEAST 4 HOURS
YIELD: 6-8 SERVINGS

½ cup honey
2 cups water
1 small cinnamon stick
1½ cups orange juice
1 cup white zinfandel wine
3 oranges
ground cinnamon

In a large saucepan, combine the honey, the water, and the cinnamon stick and bring to a boil, stirring to completely dissolve the honey. Turn down the heat and simmer until it has the consistency of a light syrup.

Remove from the heat, cool to room temperature, and discard the cinnamon stick. Stir in the orange juice and the zinfandel.

Peel the oranges deeply to remove the albedo. Carefully cut the sections from the membranes (see pages 128–129). Remove the seeds. Cut the trimmed orange sections into bite-sized pieces. Stir into the honey mixture.

Turn into a glass or china container, cover, and chill for at least 4 hours.

Ladle each serving into a soup plate or cup and dust with the cinnamon.

Mother's Sunshine Carrots

PREPARATION TIME: 15-20 MINUTES
YIELD: 4-6 SERVINGS

In Mother's original recipe, the orange juice that helps to make this side dish bright with color and rich in vitamins was added during the cooking process, but we add it the last minute to retain as much vitamin C as possible.

2 cups carrot coins
1 tablespoon sugar
1 teaspoon cornstarch
¼ teaspoon ginger
water
¼–½ cup orange juice
2 tablespoons butter or margarine
salt to taste

Cook the carrots until tender in as little water as possible. Drain, reserving the liquid, and keep the carrots warm.

In another saucepan, combine the sugar, the cornstarch, and the ginger. Stir in the reserved carrot liquid and enough water to make ½ cup. Cook the mixture until it thickens and looks somewhat clear. Stir constantly to prevent lumps.

Whisk or beat in the orange juice and the butter or margarine to make a smooth, light sauce. Pour the mixture over the reserved carrots, add the salt to taste, and serve.

California Rice

PREPARATION TIME: 25-35 MINUTES
YIELD: 4-6 SERVINGS

1 cup brown rice
2¼ cups water
¼ teaspoon nutmeg
1 orange
2 teaspoons orange zest
2 tablespoons minced parsley
salt to taste
2 tablespoons butter or margarine

In a medium covered saucepan, combine the rice, the water, and the nutmeg. Bring to a boil.

Reduce the heat to simmer, cover, and cook until tender and fluffy.

Peel and section the orange. Remove excess pith, seeds, and membrane and puree the orange sections in a blender or processor. Remove the rice from the heat. Fold in the orange puree, the orange zest, and the parsley. Add the salt to taste.

Turn the rice into a serving dish, dot with the butter or margarine, and serve.

Orange Carrot Bake

PREPARATION TIME: 5-10 MINUTES

BAKING TIME: 30 MINUTES
YIELD: 4-6 SERVINGS

¼ cup orange juice
⅛ cup honey
2 cups cooked carrots
2 tablespoons butter or margarine
2 tablespoons minced parsley
1 teaspoon lemon juice

Preheat the oven to 375°F. Butter a 1-quart covered baking dish.

Mix the orange juice with the honey in a small mixing bowl. Arrange the carrots in the baking dish, pour the orange juice mixture over the carrots, and dot with the butter or margarine.

Cover and bake for 30 minutes. Remove from the oven, sprinkle with the parsley and the lemon juice, and serve.

The Right Stuffing, Revisited

PREPARATION TIME: 10-15 MINUTES

BAKING TIME: VARIABLE
YIELD: 4-6 SERVINGS

We serve this stuffing with baked ham and sweet potatoes. It also goes well with roast chicken, turkey or duck, and is sensational tucked into lean pork chops.

1 tangerine
½ cup water chestnuts, thinly sliced
4 slices day-old bread, cubed
½ cup orange juice
¼ cup butter or margarine
⅛ cup sugar, or to taste
pinch of rosemary

Preheat the oven to 350°F. Oil a 1-quart casserole for the stuffing *or* have the fowl or chops prepared and preheat the oven to the temperature they require.

Peel the tangerine, section, and remove the seeds and excess pith. Cut the sections into bite-sized pieces, put into a large mixing bowl, and add the water chestnuts and the bread cubes.

Warm the orange juice in a small saucepan. Remove from the heat and add the butter or margarine, the sugar, and the rosemary, stirring until butter or margarine is melted and sugar is completely dissolved. Pour this mixture over the fruit mixture and toss together.

Turn the stuffing into the prepared casserole *or* spoon into the prepared fowl or chops.

Bake the stuffing for 25-30 minutes or until firm *or* roast the fowl or chops until well-done. Remove from the oven and serve.

Patatas Dulces con Naranjas

PREPARATION TIME: 10-15 MINUTES
BAKING TIME: 25-30 MINUTES
YIELD: 4-6 SERVINGS

2 cups cooked sweet potatoes or yams
2 oranges, peeled, sectioned, and trimmed
¼ cup *MIXED CITRUS MARMALADE*
  (see page 113)
¼ cup orange juice
1 teaspoon orange zest
4 tablespoons butter or margarine
1 cup miniature marshmallows

Preheat the oven to 375°F. Butter an 8-inch square baking pan.

Cut the sweet potatoes or yams into thick slices. Cut the orange sections into bite-sized pieces, removing membrane, pith, and seeds.

Arrange the potato slices and orange pieces in the baking pan.

In a small mixing bowl, blend the marmalade, the orange juice, and the orange zest. Pour this mixture over the potato slices and orange pieces, dot with the butter or margarine, and sprinkle with the marshmallows.

Bake, uncovered, until hot and bubbly and the marshmallows are a light toasty brown, about 25-30 minutes.

Remove from the oven and serve.

Right On! Relish

PREPARATION TIME: 10-15 MINUTES
CHILLING TIME: 2-4 HOURS
YIELD: ABOUT 2 CUPS

1 cup raw whole cranberries
1 small cinnamon stick
½ cup water
¾ cup sugar, or to taste
2 tangerines, peeled, sectioned, and trimmed
1 teaspoon lemon zest
2 teaspoons lemon juice

In a medium saucepan, combine the cranberries and the cinnamon stick with the water. Bring to a boil, then cook over medium heat until the cranberries are tender.

Stir in the sugar and cook until a little thicker than marmalade or jam.

Cut the tangerine sections into bite-sized pieces. Stir the tangerine pieces, the lemon zest, and the lemon juice into the cranberries. Remove from the heat and let cool to room temperature.

Turn into a covered glass or plastic container. Chill for at least 2 hours before serving.

Oranged Carrots à la Holtville

PREPARATION TIME: 15-20 MINUTES
YIELD: 4-6 SERVINGS

As authors of THE CARROT COOKBOOK, *we were invited to Holtville, California, not long ago to judge the annual Carrot Cook-off. Along with a grand tour of the town, the carrot fields, and a processing plant, we were given a 50-pound bag of those bright orange vegetables. This recipe only calls for one pound of carrots, so the rest ended up in dishes like* SWEET CARROTY, CARROTY CRACK-ERY MEATLOAF, *and dozens more. (See* THE CARROT COOKBOOK, *Garden Way Publishing.)*

1 pound carrots
water
1 teaspoon orange zest
1 orange, peeled, sectioned, and trimmed
1 tablespoon butter or margarine
1 tablespoon chopped chives
salt and pepper to taste

Wash the carrots, scrape or peel them, and cook in a covered saucepan in as little water as possible until tender. Cut the orange into bite-sized pieces.

Turn the heat to its lowest setting. Stir in the orange zest, the orange pieces, the butter or margarine, and the chives.

Mix well, add the salt and pepper to taste, and serve.

Florida-Style Baked Beans

PREPARATION TIME: 35-40 MINUTES
YIELD: 6-8 SERVINGS

1 orange
1 tablespoon butter or margarine
1 green onion, minced
2 tablespoons catsup or chili sauce
1 tablespoon molasses
1 teaspoon orange zest
3 cups baked beans

Peel, section, and trim the orange over a small bowl so that no juice is lost. Cut the sections into bite-sized pieces. Set aside.

Heat the butter or margarine in a medium saucepan and sauté the onion until limp. Stir in the catsup or chili sauce, the molasses, the orange zest, and the orange juice collected while sectioning the fruit.

Add the baked beans, cover, and cook over very low heat for 25-30 minutes. Stir occasionally to keep from sticking.

Fold the reserved orange pieces into the beans, remove from the heat, and serve.

Sweet Beets

PREPARATION TIME: 10-15 MINUTES
YIELD: 4-6 SERVINGS

½ cup orange juice
2 tablespoons brown sugar
1 teaspoon cornstarch
2 cups cooked red beets
1 tablespoon butter or margarine
salt to taste

Combine the orange juice, the brown sugar, and the cornstarch in a medium saucepan and cook over low heat, stirring constantly until the mixture has thickened to the consistency of a medium white sauce.

Fold in the beets and heat through. Stir in the butter or margarine, check the seasoning, and add the salt to taste.

Turn the beets into a bowl and serve.

Stuffed Acorn Squash

PREPARATION TIME: 10-15 MINUTES
BAKING TIME: 30-45 MINUTES
YIELD: 4 SERVINGS

2 acorn squash
1-2 oranges
½ lemon
8 tablespoons brown sugar
4 tablespoons dark rum
4 tablespoons butter or margarine
4 tablespoons coarsely chopped pecans
salt and pepper to taste

Preheat the oven to 375°F. Have ready a large, shallow baking dish.

Wash the acorn squash, cut in two lengthwise, and scoop out the seeds. Arrange the halves, cut side up, in the baking dish. Do not peel the oranges and the lemon. Cut into thick slices and remove all seeds and excess pith.

Place 2 orange slices and 1 lemon slice in each squash half. Save any remaining fruit for other uses.

Put 2 tablespoons of the brown sugar, 1 tablespoon of the rum, 1 tablespoon of the butter or margarine, and 1 tablespoon of the pecans — in that order — on top of the fruit slices in the squash halves. Salt and pepper to taste.

Cover the baking dish with foil. Tightly crimp the edges. Bake for 30-45 minutes or until tender.

Remove from the oven and serve.

PREPARATION TIME: 15–20 MINUTES
BAKING TIME: 45–60 MINUTES
YIELD: THREE 5¼-INCH LOAVES

Limey Loaf

¾ cup sugar
2 tablespoons butter or margarine, softened
1 egg
1½ cups milk
3 tablespoons lime zest
2 cups all-purpose flour
½ cup whole wheat flour
2¾ teaspoons baking powder
½ teaspoon cinnamon
½ teaspoon nutmeg
½ teaspoon salt, or to taste
¾ cup finely chopped English walnuts

Preheat the oven to 350°F. Oil and flour the loaf pans.

In a large mixing bowl, cream together the sugar and the butter or margarine. Beat the egg into the mixture, add the milk and the lime zest, then blend thoroughly.

Blend the flours, the baking powder, the spices, and the salt, then add to the egg mixture. Mix just until moistened. Fold in the nuts.

Turn the batter into the prepared loaf pans and bake for 45–60 minutes, or until golden brown on top and a tester inserted in the center comes out clean.

Remove from the oven and cool the loaves in the pans for 10 minutes. Remove from the pans, cool completely on a rack, and serve.

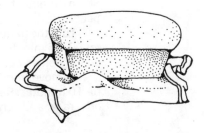

Orange Raisin Bread

PREPARATION TIME: 15-20 MINUTES
BAKING TIME: 45-60 MINUTES
YIELD: ONE 7½-INCH LOAF

4 tablespoons butter or margarine, softened
½ cup brown sugar, packed
1 egg
¾ cup orange juice
3 tablespoons grated orange peel
2¼ cups all-purpose flour
¼ teaspoon baking soda
2¼ teaspoons baking powder
¼ teaspoon salt, or to taste
1 cup raisins

Preheat the oven to 350°F. Oil and flour the loaf pan.

Cream the butter or margarine with the sugar in a small mixing bowl. Add the egg, the orange juice, and the orange peel and beat thoroughly.

Combine the flour, the baking soda, the baking powder, and the salt in a large bowl. Stir in the orange juice mixture. Fold in the raisins.

Turn the batter into the prepared loaf pan and bake for 45–60 minutes, or until a tester inserted in the center comes out clean.

Remove from the oven and cool the loaf in the pan for 10 minutes. Remove from the pan, cool completely on a rack, and serve.

Banana Bread

PREPARATION TIME: 15-20 MINUTES
BAKING TIME: 60-75 MINUTES
YIELD: ONE 8½-INCH LOAF

2 ripe bananas, mashed
2 eggs
½ cup vegetable oil
1 cup granulated sugar
½ cup brown sugar, packed
⅓ cup orange juice
1 tablespoon grated orange peel
1 teaspoon pure orange extract
1¾ cups all-purpose flour
1 teaspoon baking soda
½ teaspoon salt, or to taste
1 cup chopped pecans

Preheat the oven to 325°F. Oil and flour the loaf pan.

In a large mixing bowl, cream together the bananas, the eggs, the oil, and both sugars. Blend in the orange juice, the orange peel, and the orange extract. Stir in the flour, the baking soda, and the salt. Fold in the pecans.

Turn the batter into the prepared loaf pan and bake for 60–75 minutes, or until a cake tester inserted in the center comes out clean.

Remove from the oven and cool the loaf in the pan for 10 minutes. Remove from the pan, cool completely on a rack, and serve.

Color-Me-Orange Bread

PREPARATION TIME: 15-20 MINUTES
BAKING TIME: 60-75 MINUTES
YIELD: ONE 8½-INCH LOAF

½ cup apricot nectar
½ cup orange juice
2 tablespoons butter or margarine, softened
¾ cup coarsely chopped apricots (fresh or canned)
2 tablespoons grated orange peel
2 cups all-purpose flour
⅓ cup dark brown sugar, packed
2¼ teaspoons baking powder
¼ teaspoon baking soda
dash of salt, or to taste
½ cup chopped pecans
1 egg, beaten

Preheat the oven to 350°F. Oil and flour the loaf pan.

In a medium saucepan, bring the apricot nectar and the orange juice just to a boil. Remove from the heat and stir in the butter or margarine until melted. Add the apricot pieces and the orange peel and set aside to cool to lukewarm.

Combine the flour, the brown sugar, the baking powder, the baking soda, and the salt in a large mixing bowl. Add the pecans. Set aside.

When the apricot mixture is lukewarm, add the egg and beat well. Pour this combination over the reserved flour mixture and blend together.

Turn the batter into the prepared loaf pan and bake for 60–75 minutes, or until a tester inserted in the center comes out clean.

Remove from the oven and cool the loaf in the pan for 10 minutes. Remove from the pan, cool completely on a rack, and serve.

Minute-Mix

PREPARATION TIME: 10-15 MINUTES
YIELD: 7-8 CUPS

We make this up in a large batch, put it in a covered plastic container, and store it in the refrigerator. MINUTE-MIX can be used for such baked goods as pancakes, waffles, biscuits, muffins, and coffee cakes and can be doubled easily.

3 cups all-purpose flour
2 cups whole wheat flour
1 cup nonfat dry milk powder
⅛ cup sugar
3½ tablespoons baking powder
½ tablespoon salt, or to taste
½ tablespoon cream of tartar
1 cup butter or margarine

In a large mixing bowl, combine the flours, the dry milk powder, the sugar, the baking powder, the salt, and the cream of tartar. Mix together well.

Using a pastry knife, cut in the butter or margarine until the ingredients have the consistency of cornmeal.

Store in an airtight container in the refrigerator. It keeps indefinitely.

Honey Nut Bread

PREPARATION TIME: 15-20 MINUTES
BAKING TIME: 60-75 MINUTES
YIELD: TWO 8½-INCH LOAVES

5 cups all-purpose flour
1 teaspoon baking soda
1 teaspoon salt, or to taste
5 teaspoons baking powder
4 tablespoons butter or margarine
2 cups honey
2 eggs, well beaten
1½ cups orange juice
1½ cups chopped English walnuts

Preheat the oven to 350°F. Oil and flour the loaf pans.

Combine the flour, the baking soda, the salt, and the baking powder and set aside. In a large mixing bowl, blend the butter or margarine with the honey, the eggs, and the orange juice. Add the reserved flour mixture, stirring just until thoroughly moistened. Fold in the walnuts.

Turn the batter into the prepared loaf pans. Bake for 60-75 minutes, or until a tester inserted in the center comes out clean.

Remove from the oven and cool the loaves in the pans for 10 minutes. Remove from the pans, cool completely on a rack, and serve.

Highland Flings

PREPARATION TIME: 10-15 MINUTES
BAKING TIME: 25-30 MINUTES
YIELD: 12 MUFFINS (2¼-INCH TINS)

1 orange
⅔ cup water or milk
2 eggs
2 cups *MINUTE-MIX* (see page 75)
1 cup raw oatmeal, quick-cooking or old-fashioned
½ cup dark brown sugar, packed
1 teaspoon cinnamon
1 cup chopped dried apples

Preheat the oven to 400°F. Oil or line the muffin tins.

Cut the orange into quarters. Remove the stem end, the center strip of pith, and the seeds. Chop the quarters, peel and all, in a food chopper or processor.

Combine the chopped orange with the water or milk and the eggs in a large mixing bowl. Beat together thoroughly.

Blend the *MINUTE-MIX*, the oatmeal, the brown sugar, and the cinnamon, and stir into the egg mixture. Fold in the dried apples.

Spoon the batter into the prepared muffin tins until two-thirds full. Bake for 25-30 minutes, or until golden brown on top and the centers are firm.

Remove from the oven and serve.

Black Walnut Bread

PREPARATION TIME: 20-25 MINUTES
BAKING TIME: 45-60 MINUTES
YIELD: TWO 7½-INCH LOAVES

This delicious bread features orange juice, orange peel, and the unique flavor of black walnuts.

1½ cups all-purpose flour
1½ cups whole wheat flour
3 teaspoons baking powder
1 teaspoon cinnamon
1 egg
3 tablespoons butter or margarine, softened
¼ cup orange juice
2 tablespoons grated orange peel
1 cup milk
½ cup honey
¾ cup chopped black walnuts

Preheat the oven to 350°F. Oil and flour the loaf pans.

Stir together the flours, the baking powder, and the cinnamon in a large mixing bowl. Set aside.

In another bowl, beat together the egg and the butter or margarine. Blend in the orange juice, the orange peel, the milk, and the honey.

Combine the reserved flour mixture and the orange juice mixture and stir just until moistened. Fold in the walnuts.

Turn the batter into the prepared loaf pans. Bake for 45-60 minutes, or until a tester inserted in the center comes out clean.

Remove from the oven and cool the loaves in the pans for 10 minutes. Remove from the pans, cool completely on a rack, and serve.

Candied Fruit Muffins

PREPARATION TIME: 10-15 MINUTES
BAKING TIME: 20-25 MINUTES
YIELD: 16 MUFFINS (1½-INCH TINS)

2 eggs
¾ cup milk
⅓ cup vegetable oil
½ teaspoon salt, or to taste
¼ cup sugar
1 cup all-purpose flour
¾ cup whole wheat flour
2 teaspoons baking powder
¾ cup candied citron mix

Preheat the oven to 400°F. Oil or line the muffin tins.

Combine the eggs, the milk, the oil, the salt, and the sugar in a large mixing bowl. Blend thoroughly, then stir in the flours and the baking powder. Add the citron mix.

Spoon the batter into the prepared muffin tins until two-thirds full. Bake for 20-25 minutes, or until golden brown on top and the centers are firm.

Remove from the oven and serve.

Orange Muffins

PREPARATION TIME: 10–15 MINUTES
BAKING TIME: 15–20 MINUTES
YIELD: 12 MUFFINS (2¼-INCH TINS)

Just out of the oven, steaming and fragrant, these bright orange muffins are some of our favorites.

½ cup orange juice
¼ cup milk
¼ cup vegetable oil
2 tablespoons grated orange peel
¼ cup sugar
½ teaspoon salt, or to taste
2 eggs
1¾ cups all-purpose flour
2 teaspoons baking powder
½ cup raisins
¼ cup coarsely chopped nuts

Preheat the oven to 400°F. Oil or line the muffin tins.

In a large mixing bowl, beat together the orange juice, the milk, the oil, the orange peel, the sugar, the salt, and the eggs. Stir in the flour and the baking powder until moistened. Fold in the raisins and the nuts.

Spoon the batter into the prepared muffin tins until two-thirds full. Bake for 15–20 minutes, or until golden brown on top and the centers are firm.

Remove from the oven and serve.

Petit Pain

PREPARATION TIME: 10–15 MINUTES
BAKING TIME: 20–25 MINUTES
YIELD: 12 MUFFINS (2¼-INCH TINS)

4 teaspoons butter or margarine
12 teaspoons dark brown sugar
12 teaspoons coarsely chopped pecans
¾ cup plain low-fat yogurt
⅓ cup orange pulp
1 teaspoon orange zest
2 eggs
¼ cup sugar
2½ cups *MINUTE-MIX* (see page 75)

Preheat the oven to 400°F. Oil or line the muffin tins and put ⅓ teaspoon of the butter or margarine, 1 teaspoon of the dark brown sugar, and 1 teaspoon of the chopped pecans into each muffin tin.

In a medium mixing bowl, beat together the yogurt, the orange pulp, the orange zest, the eggs, and the sugar. Blend in the *MINUTE-MIX* just until the dry ingredients are moistened. Spoon the batter into the prepared muffin tins until two-thirds full. Bake for 20–25 minutes, or until golden brown on top and the centers are firm.

Remove from the oven and invert the muffins over a serving plate. Let stand for 1 minute, then serve hot.

Muffins Tangier

PREPARATION TIME: 10-15 MINUTES
BAKING TIME: 20-25 MINUTES
YIELD: 12 MUFFINS (2¼-INCH TINS)

1¾ cups all-purpose flour
2 teaspoons baking powder
½ teaspoon salt, or to taste
⅓ cup brown sugar, packed
2 eggs
¼ cup milk
¼ cup vegetable oil
½ cup pureed tangerine pulp
½ cup chopped dates

Preheat the oven to 400°F. Oil or line the muffin tins.

Mix the flour, the baking powder, the salt, and the brown sugar thoroughly in a large mixing bowl. In another bowl, combine the eggs, the milk, the oil, and the tangerine pulp. Add this mixture to the flour mixture and stir together until moistened. The batter will be somewhat lumpy. Fold in the dates.

Spoon the batter into the prepared muffin tins until two-thirds full. Bake for 20-25 minutes, or until golden brown on top and the centers are firm.

Remove from the oven and serve.

Grapefruit Coffeecake

PREPARATION TIME: 10-15 MINUTES
BAKING TIME: 30-45 MINUTES
YIELD: 8-10 SERVINGS

1 grapefruit, peeled, sectioned, and trimmed
¼ cup grapefruit juice
⅓ cup butter or margarine, softened
⅓ cup sugar
⅓ cup milk
1 egg, beaten
2 cups *MINUTE-MIX* (see page 75)
½ cup raisins
2 tablespoons butter or margarine, melted
2 tablespoons brown sugar
½ teaspoon cinnamon

Preheat the oven to 400°F. Oil an 8 x 8 x 8-inch baking pan.

Prepare the grapefruit in a small bowl, removing the membranes that separate the sections. Measure the ¼ cup of grapefruit juice from the sectioned grapefruit. Set the juice aside.

In a large mixing bowl, cream together the softened butter or margarine and the sugar. Beat in the milk, the egg, and the reserved grapefruit juice, then stir in the *MINUTE-MIX* and the raisins. Mix just until moistened.

Turn the batter into the prepared baking pan. Arrange the grapefruit sections on top and drizzle the melted butter or margarine over them. Combine the brown sugar and the cinnamon and sprinkle over the batter. Bake for 30-45 minutes, or until a tester inserted in the center comes out clean.

Remove from the oven and serve.

Grapefruit Chiffon Cake

PREPARATION TIME: 15-20 MINUTES
BAKING TIME: 65-75 MINUTES
YIELD: ONE 10-INCH TUBE CAKE

The first time we made this cake, it was something of a disaster, aesthetically. When we turned the tube pan upside down to cool it in the time-honored manner, the cake fell apart. Never daunted, we whipped up a bowlful of GRAPEFRUIT BUTTER CREAM FROSTING (see page 97) and used it as a mortar to hold the pieces and chunks of cake together. The next time around we came up with the recipe as it is given here and we haven't had to get out our trowels and hods since.

2¼ cups all-purpose flour
1½ cups sugar
3 teaspoons baking powder
1 teaspoon salt, or to taste
½ cup vegetable oil
5 egg yolks
¾ cup grapefruit juice
1 cup egg whites (it usually takes the whites of 8 eggs)
½ teaspoon cream of tartar

Preheat the oven to 325°F. Have ready a 10-inch tube pan.

In a large mixing bowl, combine the flour, the sugar, the baking powder, and the salt, blending thoroughly.

Make a well in the center of the flour mixture and pour in the oil, the egg yolks, and the grapefruit juice. Beat until perfectly smooth and creamy.

Combine the egg whites and the cream of tartar in a medium mixing bowl and beat the whites until they form very stiff peaks. Fold gently into the flour mixture until blended and the batter is light and smooth.

Turn the batter into the ungreased tube pan and bake for 55 minutes at 325°F, and then for 10 minutes at 350°F.

Test the center of the cake at this point and, if still too soft, leave in the oven until fully done. When done, remove from the oven, invert the pan, and cool completely.

When cool, loosen the bottom with a spatula and rap the center cone sharply on the countertop to loosen the cake.

Frost the cake with GRAPEFRUIT BUTTER CREAM FROSTING (see page 97) and serve.

Downside-Up Cake

1 can mandarin oranges
2 tablespoons butter or margarine
½ cup brown sugar, packed
½ cup chopped pecans
1 tablespoon lemon juice
yellow 1-layer cake mix
orange juice
whipped cream

Preheat the oven to 350°F. Have ready a glass 9-inch pie pan.

Drain the mandarin oranges, reserving the juice. Set aside. In the pie pan, melt the butter or margarine in the oven. When the butter or margarine is melted, remove from the oven and sprinkle with the brown sugar.

Arrange the mandarin slices in a flower petal design over the brown sugar and sprinkle with the pecans and the lemon juice.

Prepare the cake mix according to package directions using the reserved mandarin orange juice as part of the required liquid. Turn the batter into the pie pan and spread evenly over the mandarin slices, being careful not to disarrange your design.

Bake for 45-60 minutes, or until the center of the cake springs back when pressed lightly.

Remove from the oven and cool in the pan for 5 minutes, then invert the pan onto a serving plate. Serve warm with a bowl of whipped cream on the side.

Aunt Vi's Lemon Tube Cake

PREPARATION TIME: 15-20 MINUTES
BAKING TIME: 45-60 MINUTES
YIELD: ONE 10-INCH TUBE CAKE

1 cup butter or margarine, softened
½ cup solid vegetable shortening, softened
¾ cup sugar
3 eggs
1 cup sour cream
2½ cups all-purpose flour
3 teaspoons baking powder
1 teaspoon baking soda
1 teaspoon pure vanilla extract
¼ cup grated lemon peel
1 cup chopped nuts
½ cup brown sugar, packed
1 teaspoon cinnamon

Preheat the oven to 350°F. Have ready a 10-inch tube pan.

Cream and mix the butter or margarine, the shortening, the sugar, the eggs, and the sour cream in a large mixing bowl.

Blend in the flour, the baking powder, the baking soda, and the vanilla. Stir and fold until smooth and creamy.

Combine the lemon peel, the nuts, the brown sugar, and the cinnamon in a small mixing bowl and set aside.

Turn half of the batter into the prepared pan. Sprinkle with half of the reserved nut mixture. Add the rest of the batter and sprinkle with the rest of the nut mixture. Bake for 45-60 minutes, or until a tester inserted in the center comes out clean.

Remove from the oven, invert the pan, and cool completely. When cool, loosen the bottom with a spatula and rap the center cone sharply on the countertop to loosen the cake.

Frost the cake and serve.

Lemon Torte

PREPARATION TIME: 25–30 MINUTES
CHILLING TIME: AT LEAST 4 HOURS
YIELD: 12 SERVINGS

2¼ cups sugar
¼ cup cornstarch
¼ cup all-purpose flour
2¼ cups hot water
3 eggs, beaten
3 tablespoons butter or margarine
1 teaspoon lemon zest
½ cup lemon juice
1 pound or sponge loaf cake
whipped cream

Lightly butter a 2-quart soufflé pan or 8½-inch loaf pan.

Mix the sugar, the cornstarch, and the flour in a large saucepan. Gradually stir in the hot water and bring quickly to a boil, stirring constantly to prevent lumps.

Reduce the heat and continue cooking and stirring the filling until creamy and smooth.

Stir a small amount of the filling into the beaten eggs, then stir this combination into the remaining filling.

Bring the filling again to a boil and cook until thick, stirring constantly.

Remove from the heat and add the butter or margarine and the lemon zest. Stir in the lemon juice. Cool the filling to lukewarm.

Cut the pound or sponge cake into thin slices and line the bottom and sides of the baking pan with the slices, trimming to fit.

Pour one-third of the cooled filling over the cake slices. Cover the filling with a layer of cake slices trimmed to fit. Top with another third of the filling; add another layer of cake slices. Top with the remaining filling and make a "lid" of cake slices. Cover the torte with foil or plastic wrap and chill for at least 4 hours.

Invert the baking pan over a plate and let stand for a few minutes. Tap lightly on the bottom to dislodge the torte. Swirl whipped cream over the top and serve.

Orange Nut Cake

PREPARATION TIME: 20-25 MINUTES
BAKING TIME: 60-75 MINUTES
YIELD: ONE 10-INCH TUBE CAKE

1 cup butter or margarine, softened
1 cup sugar
1 cup brown sugar, packed
1 teaspoon cinnamon
1 teaspoon nutmeg
4 tablespoons grated orange peel, separated
4 eggs
1½ teaspoons pure orange extract
2 cups grated carrots
½ cup chopped nuts
3 cups all-purpose flour
3 teaspoons baking powder
½ teaspoon salt, or to taste
⅔ cup orange juice
ORANGE GLAZE (see page 97)

Preheat the oven to 350°F. Have ready a 10-inch tube pan.

In a large mixing bowl, cream together the butter or margarine and the sugars. Add the spices and 2 table-spoons of the orange peel.

Beat in the eggs one at a time, then stir in the orange extract, the carrots, and the nuts.

In another large bowl, mix together the flour, the baking powder, and the salt. Add this mixture alternately with the orange juice to the egg mixture and blend until smooth and creamy.

Turn the batter into the prepared pan and bake for 60–75 minutes, or until a tester inserted in the center comes out clean.

Remove from the oven, invert the pan, and cool completely. When cool, loosen the bottom with a spatula and rap the center cone sharply on the countertop to loosen the cake. Turn the cake onto a serving dish.

Spoon the *ORANGE GLAZE* over the top and let it run down the sides of the cake. Garnish with the orange peel and serve in thin slices.

Lemon Wafers

PREPARATION TIME: 10-15 MINUTES
BAKING TIME: 15-18 MINUTES
YIELD: 6-7 DOZEN WAFERS

These understated little cookies remind us of the vanilla wafers we used to like as children. They are not highly flavored, they don't have nubbly things like raisins and nuts in them, and the more you eat, the better they taste. We make several batches of the dough at a time, form it into rolls, wrap in plastic, freeze, and then bake a couple of sheets full whenever we feel wafer withdrawal symptoms coming on.

1 cup butter or margarine, softened
1½ cups sugar
zest and juice of 2 lemons
4 eggs, beaten
5-5½ cups all-purpose flour

In a large mixing bowl, cream together the butter or margarine and the sugar. Stir in the lemon zest and the lemon juice and beat in the eggs.

Add 5 cups of the flour a little at a time, beating well after each addition to make a smooth, stiff batter. Add the additional flour if necessary.

Divide the dough into fourths and form each fourth into a roll about 1½ inches in diameter. Wrap the rolls in plastic or waxed paper and place in the freezer.

When frozen, transfer the rolls of dough to airtight plastic bags or other suitable containers and store in the freezer until ready to bake.

At that time, preheat the oven to 350°F and oil one or more cookie sheets.

Remove a roll of dough from the freezer and, using a very sharp knife, slice into thin rounds and place on the cookie sheet. Bake for about 15 minutes or until light golden brown.

Remove from the oven and cool on racks before serving or storing.

Lemonut Balls

PREPARATION TIME: 10-15 MINUTES
BAKING TIME: 15-20 MINUTES
YIELD: ABOUT 5 DOZEN SMALL COOKIES

1 cup butter or margarine, softened
1 cup sugar
2 eggs, beaten
2½ tablespoons lemon juice
2 tablespoons lemon zest
1 cup whole wheat flour
1 cup all-purpose flour
½ cup broken English walnut meats

Preheat the oven to 350°F. Oil one or two cookie sheets.

In a large mixing bowl, cream the butter or margarine with the sugar. Stir in the eggs, the lemon juice, and the lemon zest and blend thoroughly. Add the flours to make a smooth, fairly stiff dough.

Place a teaspoonful of the dough at a time on prepared cookie sheets, leaving about a 1½-inch clearance around the dough. Press a piece of nutmeat into each bit of dough. Bake for 15-20 minutes or until rich golden brown.

Remove from the oven and cool on racks before serving or storing.

Treasure Chest Cookies

PREPARATION TIME: 10-15 MINUTES
BAKING TIME: 7-10 MINUTES
YIELD: ABOUT 5½ DOZEN MEDIUM COOKIES

These cookies are well named: They're so good you may be tempted to stash them in your safe deposit box to keep them out of the reach of cookie pirates large and small. We've made them time and again and every batch is right on the money — light, luscious, and lively.

½ cup butter or margarine, softened
1 cup sugar
1 egg, beaten
½ cup orange juice
¼ cup grated orange peel
2 cups all-purpose flour
1 teaspoon cream of tartar
½ teaspoon baking soda

Preheat the oven to 350°F. Oil one or two cookie sheets.

Cream the butter or margarine with the sugar in a large mixing bowl. Beat in the egg, the orange juice, and the orange peel and mix thoroughly.

Combine the flour, the cream of tartar, and the baking soda and add to the orange juice mixture, blending well.

Spoon the batter by teaspoonsful onto the prepared cookie sheets and bake for 7-10 minutes or until light golden brown.

Remove from the oven and cool on racks before serving or storing.

Tangerola Bars

1 medium tangerine
⅓ cup butter or margarine
¾ cup dark brown sugar, packed
2 cups quick-cooking raw oatmeal
½ cup raisins
1 teaspoon cinnamon
¼ teaspoon salt, or to taste

Preheat the oven to 350°F. Lightly oil an 8 x 8 x 2-inch baking pan.

Peel and section the tangerine, working over a bowl or plate so none of the juice is lost. Remove the seeds and cut the sections into bite-sized pieces. Set aside.

Mix the butter or margarine and the brown sugar in a small saucepan and set over low heat, stirring occasionally.

Combine the raw oatmeal, the raisins, the cinnamon, and the salt in a large mixing bowl, then add the reserved tangerine pieces. Toss all the ingredients together until thoroughly mixed.

Remove the butter mixture from the heat and pour over the oatmeal mixture until all ingredients are coated, but still crumbly.

Turn the mixture into the baking pan and press firmly and evenly to cover the bottom of the pan.

Bake for 25-30 minutes or until a rich golden brown on the edges.

Remove from the oven and cut into bars while still hot. Cool in the pan, and serve.

Apple and Orange Bars

½ cup butter or margarine, softened
½ cup sugar
1 cup all-purpose flour
1 orange, peeled, trimmed, and sectioned
2 eggs
2 medium apples, cored, peeled, and sliced
1 cup brown sugar, packed
½ cup chopped nuts
½ teaspoon cinnamon
1 teaspoon orange zest
2 tablespoons all-purpose flour
½ teaspoon baking powder

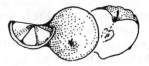

Preheat the oven to 400°F. Lightly oil an 8 x 8 x 2-inch baking pan.

Cream together the butter or margarine and the sugar in a large mixing bowl. Add the 1 cup of flour and make a stiff dough.

Shape the dough into a ball and press firmly and evenly to cover the bottom of the pan. Bake for 15 minutes or until golden brown.

Cut the orange sections into small bite-sized pieces. Set aside. Beat the eggs and add the apples, the reserved orange pieces, the brown sugar, the nuts, the cinnamon, and the orange zest. Stir in the 2 tablespoons of flour and the baking powder and blend well.

When the dough is baked, spread the apple mixture evenly on top, return to the oven, and bake for 25-30 minutes, or until set on top and brown on the bottom.

Remove from the oven and cool in the pan. Cut into bars and serve.

Nut 'n' Limey Bars

PREPARATION TIME: 10-15 MINUTES
BAKING TIME: 30-35 MINUTES
YIELD: 18-24 BARS

We tested these bars so often the first few times we made them that there weren't any left by the time they were completely cooled and chilled. We finally decided we might as well double the recipe so we could have some to test and some to save. They are delicious!

2 teaspoons lime zest
⅓ cup lime juice
1 tablespoon lemon juice
1 14-ounce can sweetened condensed milk
½ cup butter or margarine, softened
½ cup dark brown sugar, packed
1½ cups whole wheat flour
1 teaspoon baking powder
½ cup chopped pecans

Preheat the oven to 325°F. Lightly oil a 12 x 7 x 2-inch baking pan.

Beat the lime zest, the lime juice, the lemon juice, and the condensed milk together in a medium mixing bowl. Set aside.

In a large mixing bowl, combine the butter or margarine and the brown sugar and cream together. Stir in the flour, the baking powder, and the pecans. Mix together until the mixture has the consistency of pie crust dough without the water.

Remove 1 cup of the flour mixture and set aside. Press the remainder evenly over the bottom of the pan. Spread the reserved lime mixture over the crust and sprinkle with the reserved cup of the flour mixture. Bake for 30-35 minutes or until golden brown.

Remove from the oven and cool in the pan, then chill for 1 hour. Cut into bars and serve.

These bars freeze well. Place in airtight plastic bags or other appropriate containers and freeze.

Pennies-From-Heaven Cookies

PREPARATION TIME: 10-15 MINUTES
BAKING TIME: 12-15 MINUTES
YIELD: ABOUT 5 DOZEN SMALL COOKIES

Forewarned is forearmed! We advise you to double this recipe today and save yourself the trouble of mixing up a second batch — tomorrow!

1 cup butter or margarine, softened
1 cup sugar
½ cup *LEMON JAM* (see page 120)
1 egg
2 cups all-purpose flour
1¾ teaspoons baking powder

Preheat the oven to 350°F. Oil one or two cookie sheets.

Cream the butter or margarine and the sugar in a large mixing bowl. Beat in the *LEMON JAM* and the egg.

Mix the flour and the baking powder together in another bowl. Add to the egg mixture and blend well.

Spoon the batter by teaspoonful onto the cookie sheets and bake the cookies for 12–15 minutes or until golden brown.

Remove from the oven and cool on racks before serving or storing.

Orange Sauce

PREPARATION TIME: 15–20 MINUTES
YIELD: ABOUT 2 CUPS

Serve this simple sauce on crumb tortes, cakes, and puddings, or use it as a filling for white, yellow or orange-flavored layer cakes.

1 egg white
1 tablespoon cornstarch
½ cup cold water
1 egg yolk, beaten
1 tablespoon butter
1 tablespoon lemon juice
4 teaspoons orange zest
⅓ cup orange juice
dash of salt, or to taste
½ cup sugar, or to taste

Beat the egg white in a small mixing bowl until stiff peaks form. Set aside.

Combine the cornstarch and the water in a medium saucepan and cook until smooth and thick. Gradually stir the egg yolk, the butter, the lemon juice, the orange zest, the orange juice, the salt, and the sugar into the cornstarch mixture.

Cook, stirring constantly, until it has the consistency of a medium white sauce. Let cool to room temperature, then fold in the stiffly beaten egg white, and the sauce is ready to use.

Double Dip Sauce

PREPARATION TIME: 10–15 MINUTES
YIELD: ABOUT 2½ CUPS

This sauce is simplicity itself, and we don't think it could be better. We spoon it over ice cream, thin it slightly with a little warm water and pour it onto waffles or layer it — chilled — with vanilla pudding in tall parfait glasses with a dollop of whipped cream on top.

1 cup *MELLOW YELLOW MARMALADE*
   (see page 111)
1 cup apricot jam
½ cup water
4 tablespoons butter or margarine
⅛ cup lemon juice
¼ cup dark rum

In a blender or processor, blend the marmalade and the jam until smooth.

Turn the mixture into a medium saucepan along with the water and bring just to a boil.

Remove from the heat, stir in the butter or margarine, the lemon juice, and the rum, and the sauce is ready to use.

Fourth of July Fondue

PREPARATION TIME: 5 MINUTES
CHILLING TIME: AT LEAST 1 HOUR
YIELD: 1¼ CUPS

Unlike the cheese fondues we're used to in the autumn and winter, this creamy mixture is made for hot summer holidays.

1 cup sour cream
¼ cup powdered sugar
2 tablespoons light rum
2 teaspoons pure vanilla extract
1 tablespoon orange zest

Combine all the ingredients in a small mixing bowl, blend well, and chill for at least 1 hour.

Serve the fondue with bite-sized pieces of oranges, apples, tangerines, bananas, apricots, peaches, pears or other fruits.

Brandy and Orange Sauce

PREPARATION TIME: 5-10 MINUTES
YIELD: ABOUT 1 CUP

Serve this elegant sauce with ice cream, a blanc mange, a sponge or pound cake, a steamed pudding, thick cartwheels of deeply peeled oranges or folded into leftover rice for an instant, delicious pudding.

3 tablespoons brandy
1 tablespoon orange zest
2 egg whites
¼ teaspoon salt
1 cup powdered sugar

In a small mixing bowl, combine the brandy and the orange zest and set aside.

In a medium mixing bowl, beat the egg whites with the salt until stiff. Add the powdered sugar and continue beating until stiff peaks form.

Dribble the brandy and orange zest combination into the egg whites and fold through until smooth and coherent.

Cover and chill until ready to serve.

Light Lemon Sauce

PREPARATION TIME: 15-20 MINUTES
CHILLING TIME: AT LEAST 2 HOURS
YIELD: ABOUT 2 CUPS

½ tablespoon cornstarch
1 cup water
2 eggs
1 cup sugar
zest of 1 lemon
⅓ cup lemon juice
1 cup heavy cream

In a medium saucepan over low heat, stir the cornstarch and the water together until smooth.

Beat the eggs and the sugar together in a small mixing bowl until light and fluffy. Add gradually to the cornstarch mixture, stirring constantly to prevent lumps.

When the cornstarch mixture has thickened to the consistency of a heavy white sauce, remove from the heat and stir in the lemon zest and the lemon juice. Let cool to room temperature.

Cover and chill for at least 2 hours. When ready to use, whip the heavy cream, fold through the sauce, and serve.

Best Ever Jam Sauce

PREPARATION TIME: 10-15 MINUTES
YIELD: ABOUT 2 CUPS

This is a sauce we use often. It is light, delicate, and refreshing.

¼ cup cold water
½ cup raspberry jam
½ tablespoon cornstarch
¾ cup orange juice
⅛ cup lemon juice

Combine the water and the jam in a small saucepan, bring to a boil, and cook for 5 minutes over low heat.

In a small mixing bowl, stir the cornstarch and the orange juice together, then add, a little at a time, to the jam, stirring constantly to prevent lumps.

Bring to a boil and stir until thick. Remove from the heat and blend in the lemon juice.

Serve at once while warm, or chill and serve cold.

Bride's Cookbook Orange Frosting

PREPARATION TIME: 20-25 MINUTES
YIELD: 2-2½ CUPS

2 tablespoons orange zest
1 tablespoon orange juice
½ teaspoon lemon juice
1 egg
1½-2 cups powdered sugar

Combine the orange zest, the orange juice, and the lemon juice in a medium mixing bowl and let stand for a few minutes.

Add the egg and beat until light and frothy.

Stir in enough powdered sugar to make the frosting the right consistency for spreading.

Spread on layer cakes, cupcakes or cookies.

Pink Cream Cheese Frosting

PREPARATION TIME: 10-15 MINUTES
YIELD: 2-2½ CUPS

1 8-ounce package cream cheese, softened
1-2 cups powdered sugar
2 tablespoons pink grapefruit zest
½ teaspoon pure vanilla extract
pink grapefruit juice

Cream the cheese and 1 cup of the powdered sugar together in a medium mixing bowl. Add the grapefruit zest and the vanilla.

Add enough grapefruit juice, along with the remainder of the powdered sugar, to make the frosting light, fluffy, and the right consistency for spreading.

Spread on layer cakes, cupcakes or between graham cracker squares.

Sour Cream Frosting

PREPARATION TIME: 10-15 MINUTES
YIELD: 1½ CUPS

1 cup semisweet chocolate pieces
1 tablespoon orange zest
½ cup sour cream

Melt the chocolate pieces in the top of a double boiler or in a small pan set into a larger pan containing an inch or two of water.

When melted, remove from the heat and blend in the orange zest and the sour cream.

Cool and spread on layer cakes, cupcakes or cookies.

Lemon Glaze

PREPARATION TIME: 5-10 MINUTES
YIELD: ABOUT ½ CUP

This simple glaze — easy to mix up, easy to store, easy to spread — is good as a topping for bars, cakes, sweet rolls or cookies.

1 tablespoon lemon juice
2 tablespoons orange juice
1 cup powdered sugar

Beat all the ingredients together in a small mixing bowl. If the glaze seems too thick, add a little more orange juice. If it seems too thin, add a little more powdered sugar and the glaze is ready to use.

Grapefruit Butter Cream Frosting

PREPARATION TIME: 10-15 MINUTES
YIELD: ABOUT 1½ CUPS

The power of citrus fruit zest is proven in this recipe, where two little teaspoonsful are enough to flavor all of the other ingredients.

¼ cup butter
2 cups powdered sugar
2 teaspoons grapefruit zest
1-2 tablespoons cream

Cream the butter and the powdered sugar together in a medium mixing bowl. Beat in the grapefruit zest and the cream, 1 tablespoonful at a time, until the mixture has the right consistency for spreading.

Spread on layer cakes (see page 81), cupcakes or cookies.

Orange Glaze

PREPARATION TIME: 5-10 MINUTES
YIELD: ABOUT 1 CUP

1¼ cups powdered sugar
1 tablespoon butter or margarine, softened
1 teaspoon orange zest
1 tablespoon orange juice
orange liqueur

Combine the powdered sugar with the butter or margarine in a medium mixing bowl and blend with the orange zest and the orange juice.

Stir in enough orange liqueur to make a light glaze. Spread on cakes, cupcakes, breakfast muffins or sweet rolls.

Oranges Ganymede

4 oranges
1 cup heavy cream
1 tablespoon orange liqueur
nutmeg

Two hours before making this dessert, chill a small mixing bowl, beaters, and the cream.

Cut the oranges in half. Cut a thin slice from the base of the orange halves to give them stability. Cut around each section with a grapefruit knife and scoop out the flesh. Set aside. Remove the center core of pith and the seeds (see page 138). Reserve the orange sections and the shells.

Whip the cream. Fold in the reserved orange sections and the liqueur. Spoon the cream mixture into the orange shells.

Arrange the filled shells on a plate, cover with plastic wrap or foil, and freeze overnight.

About half an hour before serving, take the ORANGES out of the freezer so the filling can soften slightly. Garnish each shell with a sprinkle of nutmeg.

Tangerine Sorbet

1 cup sugar
1 cup water
2 large or 3 small tangerines
½ cup frozen concentrated orange juice, undiluted
½ cup lemon juice
⅓ cup heavy cream

Combine the sugar and the water in a covered sauce-pan. Bring to just under a boil, stirring constantly to completely dissolve the sugar.

Remove the sugar syrup from the heat, cool to room temperature, then cover and chill.

Remove the zest of the tangerines and mince as fine as possible. Remove and discard the rest of the peel, the pith, and the seeds. Separate the tangerine sections and puree in a processor or blender.

Stir the tangerine puree into the chilled syrup. Add the tangerine zest, the orange concentrate, and the lemon juice and blend well.

Turn the tangerine mixture into an ice-cream maker and freeze just to the soft stage. Add the cream to the tangerine mixture and complete the churning. Serve or store in a covered plastic container in the freezer.

Frozen Calico Cream

PREPARATION TIME: 15–20 MINUTES
FREEZING TIME: AT LEAST 4 HOURS
YIELD: 8–10 SERVINGS

3 tablespoons butter or margarine
3 tablespoons all-purpose flour
¾ cup low-fat milk
½ cup dark brown sugar, packed
1 egg, beaten
¼ cup lemon juice
1 3-ounce package cream cheese, softened
1 cup heavy cream, whipped
**1 cup mandarin sections, cut into bite-sized
  pieces**
½ cup peaches, cut into bite-sized pieces
½ cup pears, cut into bite-sized pieces

Lightly butter an 8 x 8 x 2-inch glass baking pan. Set aside.

In a medium saucepan, melt the butter or margarine, stir in the flour, and cook over medium heat, stirring constantly until the flour bubbles.

Add the milk and the brown sugar, stirring to prevent lumps. Beat in the egg and cook the mixture until thick and smooth.

Remove from the heat and stir in the lemon juice. Set aside to cool to room temperature.

When the mixture is cool, blend in the cream cheese until perfectly smooth.

Fold in the whipped cream and the fruits and turn the mixture into the baking dish. Cover with foil or plastic wrap. Freeze for at least 4 hours.

When ready to serve, cut into squares and arrange on individual dessert plates.

Bavarian Cream

1 envelope unflavored gelatin
½ cup cold water
1¼ cups orange, tangerine, tangelo or tangor juice
1 teaspoon orange, tangerine, tangelo or tangor zest
½ cup powdered sugar
1 tablespoon lemon juice
1 cup heavy cream
orange, tangerine, tangelo or tangor sections

Lightly oil a 1-quart mold or six individual molds. Set aside.

Sprinkle the gelatin over the cold water in a small saucepan and let stand for 5 minutes. Heat the water and the gelatin, stirring constantly, until the gelatin has completely dissolved.

Cool the gelatin to room temperature, pour into a large mixing bowl, and chill until it has the consistency of egg whites.

Remove from the refrigerator, beat until light and frothy, then add the citrus juice, the citrus zest, the powdered sugar, and the lemon juice. Mix well.

Whip the cream in a medium mixing bowl until it forms stiff peaks. Fold into the fruit mixture and turn into the prepared mold or molds.

Chill until firm. Unmold onto a serving plate or individual dessert plates, garnish with citrus sections, and serve.

Fruit Parfait

PREPARATION TIME: 10-15 MINUTES
CHILLING TIME: AT LEAST 4 HOURS
YIELD: 4 SERVINGS

1 cup pineapple chunks
1 mandarin, peeled, trimmed, sectioned, and
 diced
1 kiwifruit, peeled and sliced
1 tangerine, peeled, trimmed, and sectioned
1 banana, sliced
½ cup pineapple juice
1 cup whipped topping
½ cup chopped nuts

In a large mixing bowl, combine the pineapple chunks, the mandarin pieces, the kiwifruit slices, and the tangerine sections. Set aside.

Put the banana slices and the pineapple juice into a processor or blender and puree. Pour this mixture over the reserved fruits and fold gently together.

Cover and chill for at least 4 hours.

Spoon the chilled fruits into parfait glasses in layers alternating with the whipped topping. Sprinkle with the nuts and serve.

Mousse à l'Orange

PREPARATION TIME: 15-20 MINUTES
CHILLING TIME: 2-4 HOURS
YIELD: 8-10 SERVINGS

1 envelope unflavored gelatin
¼ cup cold water
1 cup whipping cream
1 8-ounce package cream cheese, softened
6 ounces frozen concentrated orange juice, undiluted
¾ cup powdered sugar
1 teaspoon pure vanilla extract
orange twists
mint sprigs

Combine the gelatin and the water in a blender or processor and let stand for 5 minutes.

Heat the cream to just under a boil in a small saucepan. Don't let it scorch.

Add the hot cream to the gelatin in the blender and process until the gelatin is completely dissolved.

Add the cream cheese, the orange juice concentrate, the powdered sugar, and the vanilla and process at high speed until well blended.

Turn the mixture into a pudding mold or serving dish, cover, and chill until firm. Serve, garnished with the orange twists and the mint sprigs.

Tart Terrific

PREPARATION TIME: 20-25 MINUTES   CHILLING TIME: 2 HOURS
BAKING TIME: 25 MINUTES   YIELD: ONE 15-INCH TART

This is an impressive tart — a giant pastry covered with fruits, topped off with a tangy glaze and dollops of whipped or sour cream, dusted with nutmeg.

1 recipe *RIVER INN PIE CRUST,* **enough for two 9-inch crusts (see page 106)**
1 8-ounce package cream cheese, softened
⅓ cup sugar
2 teaspoons pure vanilla extract
mandarins, tangerines, bananas, kiwifruit, peaches, pears, apricots, and pineapple
½ cup *KUMQUAT MARMALADE* (see page 116)
orange juice
whipped cream
sour cream
nutmeg

Preheat the oven to 425°F. Oil a pizza pan or cookie sheet.

Roll the dough on waxed paper to cookie thickness in a rectangle or round shape. Place on the pizza pan or cookie sheet and bake for 12–15 minutes or until golden brown. Remove from the oven and allow to cool.

Blend the cream cheese, the sugar, and the vanilla. Spread this mixture carefully on the cooled crust and arrange the slices, sections or chunks of mandarins, tangerines, bananas, kiwifruit, peaches, pears, apricots, and pineapple on the mixture.

Combine the marmalade with enough orange juice to make a medium-thin glaze. Drizzle over the fruits.

Chill for 2 hours. Cut into wedges and serve with side dishes of the whipped cream or the sour cream dusted with the nutmeg.

Ambrosia Pie

¾ cup sugar
3 tablespoons cornstarch
3 eggs, separated
2 tablespoons lemon juice
1⅔ cups orange juice
2 teaspoons orange zest
1 cup grated coconut
1 baked 9-inch pie crust

Mix the sugar and the cornstarch in a large saucepan. Beat the egg yolks, the lemon juice, the orange juice, and the orange zest together in a small mixing bowl. Add this mixture to the sugar mixture, stirring until smooth.

Cook over low heat until thick, stirring constantly to prevent lumps. Remove from the heat and cool to room temperature.

Beat the egg whites until stiff peaks form. Fold the egg whites and the coconut through the orange mixture.

Mound the filling in the pastry shell and chill for at least 2 hours before serving.

Key Lime Pie

2 cups instant nonfat dry milk powder
1⅔ cups powdered sugar
6 tablespoons margarine, softened
⅔ cup very hot water
3 egg whites
½ cup plus 2 tablespoons fresh Key lime juice
1 baked 9-inch pie crust
sour cream (optional)
whipped cream (optional)
semisweet chocolate curls (optional)

Preheat the oven to 350°F. Have ready a 9-inch pie pan.

Combine the dry milk powder, the powdered sugar, the margarine, and the water in a blender or processor and blend together.

Add the egg whites and the lime juice to the other ingredients and blend until smooth, thick, and creamy.

Turn the filling into the baked pie crust and bake for 15-20 minutes, or until the center is somewhat firm.

Remove from the oven and let stand for 10 minutes before serving, or let cool and chill.

When ready to serve the chilled pie, spread a thin layer of the sour cream over the top or swirl with the whipped cream. Shave thin curls of the semisweet chocolate lightly over the topping.

Orange Pattipans

The ancestors who came to this country on the Mayflower baked their tarts and other pastries in "pattipans." This one features a crispy crust spread with marmalade, filled with succulent mandarin sections, and swirled with whipped cream.

1½ cups all-purpose flour
½ teaspoon salt, or to taste
½ cup solid vegetable shortening
3–4 tablespoons cold water
3 cups canned mandarin sections, drained
¼ cup reserved mandarin liquid
½ cup *NOT-SO-PROPER-BRITISH MARMALADE*
   (see page 115)
whipped cream

Preheat the oven to 425°F. Have ready a 9-inch pie or tart pan.

Combine the flour, the salt, and the shortening in a medium mixing bowl. Cut the shortening in with a pastry cutter, then stir in the water with a fork to make a stiff but workable dough.

Pat the dough to fit the pan. Prick the bottom and sides with a fork to prevent bulging and puffing. Line the pastry dough with a circle of foil and fill with dried beans, raw rice or special pastry weights to keep the pastry flat.

Bake for 10 minutes, remove the foil and weights, and continue baking for about 5 more minutes or until light golden brown. Remove from the oven and cool on a wire rack.

Drain the mandarin sections and add the drained liquid to the marmalade. Set the mandarin sections aside.

Bring the marmalade mixture to a boil in a small saucepan over low heat, remove from the heat, and let cool to room temperature.

Spread half of the marmalade mixture over the bottom and sides of the crust. Arrange the reserved mandarin sections in the crust and dribble on the rest of the marmalade mixture.

Spread the whipped cream over the top of the whole *PATTIPAN*, or spoon on each piece before serving.

PREPARATION TIME: 15-20 MINUTES
BAKING TIME: 12-15 MINUTES OR MORE
YIELD: TWO 9-INCH CRUSTS

River Inn Pie Crust

Lu and Ray Conrad run The River Inn, a favorite spot for cowhands at the foot of Thousand Lakes Mountain. The Conrads told us this recipe never fails, and they were right. It's our kind of pie crust. It makes enough for two single-crust pies or one double-crust pie. Adjust the baking time if you are making a filled double-crust pie or two prebaked single crusts which will be filled later.

3 cups all-purpose flour
1½ teaspoons salt, or to taste
1½ cups solid vegetable shortening
5-6 tablespoons cold water
3 tablespoons cider vinegar
1 egg, beaten
filling (optional)

Preheat the oven to 400°F for prebaked crusts. Have ready two 9-inch pie pans.

In a large mixing bowl, blend the flour and the salt, and cut in the shortening with knives or a pastry cutter.

Combine the water, the vinegar, and the egg. Stir this mixture into the flour mixture with a fork until moistened.

Divide the dough into two parts and roll out into circles on a lightly floured board or between sheets of waxed paper.

For two single crusts, fit the pastry circles into the two pans. Prick the sides and bottoms with a fork to prevent bubbling and bulging. Line the pastry dough with a circle of foil and fill with dried beans, raw rice or special pastry weights to keep the pastry flat.

Bake the crust for 7 minutes, remove the foil and weights, and continue baking until light golden brown. Cool before adding a filling.

Mother's Lemon Meringue Pie

PREPARATION TIME: 15–20 MINUTES
YIELD: ONE 8-INCH PIE

1¼ cups sugar
3 tablespoons cornstarch
1¼ cups water
½ cup lemon juice
3 eggs, separated
1 baked 8-inch pie crust
meringue (see directions)

Combine the sugar, the cornstarch, and the water in a medium saucepan and blend well. Bring the mixture to a boil. Cook for 5 minutes on low heat, stirring constantly to prevent lumps. Stir in the lemon juice.

Stir the egg yolks — don't beat them — in a small mixing bowl. Add 2 or 3 tablespoons of the lemon mixture to the yolks. Gradually blend this mixture into the remaining lemon mixture, stirring constantly.

Continue to cook over low heat until thick. Remove from the heat and let cool to room temperature, then turn the filling into the baked pie crust.

Preheat the oven to 350°F while you prepare the MERINGUE: Beat the egg whites together with 4 tablespoons of sugar until stiff peaks form.

Spoon the egg whites over the top of the filled pie and place in the oven for 10–15 minutes, or until the peaks are golden brown.

Remove from the oven and allow to cool before serving.

Mincemeat Crisp

PREPARATION TIME: 10-15 MINUTES
BAKING TIME: 30-35 MINUTES
YIELD: 8-10 SERVINGS

1 22-ounce can prepared mincemeat pie filling
2 tablespoons grated orange peel
½ cup orange juice
1 tablespoon lemon juice
⅓ cup brown sugar, packed
1 cup quick-cooking raw oatmeal
3 tablespoons butter or margarine

Preheat the oven to 375°F. Butter an 8-inch square baking pan.

In a medium mixing bowl, blend the mincemeat, the orange peel, the orange juice, and the lemon juice. Set aside.

Combine the brown sugar and the oatmeal in another bowl. Cut in the butter or margarine with a pastry cutter or knives.

Turn the mincemeat mixture into the buttered pan and sprinkle with the oatmeal topping. Bake for 30-35 minutes, or until the filling bubbles and the crust is golden brown.

Remove from the oven and serve warm with light cream, whipped topping or ice cream.

Lime Marble

PREPARATION TIME: 10-15 MINUTES
YIELD: 6-8 SERVINGS

This pudding is so delicious we felt we had to experiment with it several times in order to make sure we had gotten it just right. We had. It also makes a superb filling for prebaked pie crusts (see page 106).

3 eggs, separated
½ cup freshly squeezed lime juice
1 14-ounce can sweetened condensed milk
1 cup heavy cream, chilled

Beat the egg whites in a large mixing bowl until stiff peaks form. Set aside.

Combine the lime juice, the milk, and the egg yolks in a blender or processor and blend until perfectly smooth and thickened slightly.

Fold the lime mixture through the reserved egg whites until completely blended.

Whip the cream and swirl through the pudding, leaving streaks of white cream showing to give a delicate marbled effect.

Serve, or chill and serve cold.

Carrot Pudding

PREPARATION TIME: 15-20 MINUTES
BAKING TIME: 50-60 MINUTES
YIELD: 6-8 SERVINGS

2-3 oranges
½ cup grated carrots
1 teaspoon orange zest
1 large egg
¾ cup sugar
1 cup all-purpose flour
½ teaspoon baking soda
⅛ teaspoon salt, or to taste
½ teaspoon cinnamon
¼ teaspoon ginger
½ cup instant nonfat dry milk powder
¾ cup water
¼ cup melted butter or margarine
1 teaspoon pure orange extract

Preheat the oven to 325°F. Butter a 1½-quart baking pan or ovenproof dish.

Peel, trim, seed, and section the oranges. Puree in a blender or processor to make 1 cup of pulp.

Combine the orange pulp with the grated carrots and the orange zest in a medium mixing bowl. Beat in the egg and the sugar.

In another mixing bowl, stir together the flour, the baking soda, the salt, the cinnamon, the ginger, and the dry milk powder. Add this combination to the orange mixture with the water, the butter or margarine, and the orange extract.

Blend thoroughly and turn the batter into the prepared baking pan or dish.

Bake for 50-60 minutes, or until a knife inserted in the center comes out clean. Remove from the oven and serve warm, with light cream or your favorite sauce (see pages 93-95).

California Custard

3 eggs
⅓ cup sugar
⅛ teaspoon salt, or to taste
½ cup orange juice
1½ cups whole milk
½ cup chopped nuts
nutmeg

Preheat the oven to 325°F. Put a shallow pan of hot water into the oven. Lightly butter individual custard cups or a 1-quart baking dish.

Beat the eggs in a large mixing bowl until frothy and lemon-colored. Add the sugar and the salt and continue beating until thick. Gradually add the orange juice and the milk to the egg mixture and blend well.

Pour into the prepared cups or baking dish and place in the shallow pan of hot water and bake for 45–60 minutes, or until a knife inserted in the center comes out clean.

Remove from the oven and sprinkle with the nuts and a light dusting of nutmeg. Serve warm, or cool to room temperature, chill, and serve cold.

Mellow Yellow Marmalade

PREPARATION TIME: 20–30 MINUTES   STANDING TIME: 18 HOURS
COOKING TIME: 2–4 HOURS   YIELD: 6–7 CUPS

This marmalade is unusual because there is not an orange to be found in it — only yellow grapefruit, yellow pineapple, and yellow lemon. The finished product is, not surprisingly, a lovely warm deep yellow color with a wonderful unique flavor.

3 medium yellow grapefruit
1 lemon
1 15¼-ounce can crushed pineapple
1½ cups water
2 teaspoons pure vanilla extract
4–5 cups sugar

Wash and sterilize seven half-pint jelly glasses, jam pots or canning jars and lids.

Wash the grapefruit and lemon and cut off the stem ends. Cut the fruits into very thin slices and the slices into eight wedges.

Combine the citrus wedges with the pineapple, the juice from the can, and the water in a large glass or china container. Cover and let stand for 12 hours or overnight.

Pour the fruit mixture into a large stainless steel saucepan and boil for 15 minutes. Turn off the heat, cover, and let stand for 6 hours.

Measure the fruit mixture, add the vanilla, and 3 cups of sugar for every 4 cups of fruit and liquid. Return the mixture to the saucepan and bring to a boil.

Stir constantly until the sugar is completely dissolved. Continue to boil, stirring occasionally, until the marmalade sheets from a metal spoon (see pages 112–113).

When the marmalade sheets, cool slightly, then ladle into the prepared jars. Seal and process according to manufacturer's directions.

Lovers' Marmalade

PREPARATION TIME: 30 MINUTES
COOKING TIME: 4–6 HOURS

SOAKING TIME: 48 HOURS
YIELD: 12–14 CUPS

We found the recipe for this marmalade in a cookbook that was given to Grandma and Grandpa Hendrickson when they were married, back in the early days of this century. We're not certain whether the title means it's marmalade for lovers, per se, or marmalade for marmalade lovers.

The recipe makes a lot! Ordinarily, we cut amounts in half and still get 6–7 cups — enough for our own needs, gifts to friends, and storage for later use.

**3 oranges
2 grapefruit
2 lemons
water
sugar**

Wash and sterilize fourteen half-pint jelly glasses, jam pots or canning jars and lids.

Choose whole, perfect grapefruit, oranges, and lemons; wash carefully and cut a thin slice, which we discard, off both ends of each fruit. Cut the fruits into the thinnest slices possible.

This is the hardest part of marmalade-making. Once this task is done, it's more watching and waiting than work. A very sharp long-bladed knife is a must. Slice on a board set on a plate so that none of the juice is lost. It takes 20–30 minutes to do the job by hand. Using a food processor, the fruits could be prepared in a few minutes.

Soak the fruits in a large glass mixing bowl covered with plastic wrap.

After the first 24-hour period, transfer the soaked fruits to a large stainless steel pot and simmer for 15 minutes. Let cool, and return to the glass bowl for the second 24-hour soaking period.

At the end of that time, measure the fruit and water mixture and add ¾ as much sugar as fruit and water. Pour the mixture back into the stainless steel pot for the second, and final, cooking.

Bring the mixture to a rolling boil, stirring constantly until the sugar is completely dissolved, then stir occasionally to prevent sticking and burning.

The original recipe directions called for boiling the marmalade until it jelled. Test for that critical moment by regularly stirring the mixture in a figure-eight movement with a metal spoon, holding the stirring spoon over the pot, and observing the manner in which the syrup flows off the spoon. (To reach the jelling stage, it will take at least two hours.)

At first the syrup flow is thin and water-like, but after more cooking it begins to thicken and leave the edge of the spoon in globules, instead of in a steady flow. This means that the marmalade is getting close to the jelling stage.

Stay close to the pot now. Stir and check the syrup often. Finally, when it "sheets" off the edge of the spoon (you'll recognize what that "sheeting" is when you see it), remove from the heat.

Carefully ladle the hot marmalade into the prepared jelly glasses, jam pots or canning jars and pro-

ceed according to canning and/or freezing directions provided with the jars. Can or freeze the marmalade you don't use within the next few weeks.

If you find you have misjudged the jelling stage and the marmalade is too runny, simply return the marmalade to the pot and cook until it does sheet properly from the spoon.

If the marmalade has become too thick, return the marmalade to the pot, add a small amount of water, and bring it back to a boil.

Rewash and resterilize the jelly glasses, jam pots or jars with **new** lids and proceed according to directions above.

Mixed Citrus Marmalade

PREPARATION TIME: 20-30 MINUTES
COOKING TIME: 2-3 HOURS

STANDING TIME: 18 HOURS
YIELD: 3 CUPS

1 orange
1 tangerine
1 lemon
1 lime
6 cups water
sugar

Wash and sterilize three half-pint jelly glasses, jam pots or canning jars and lids.

Wash the fruits and cut off the stem ends. Cut the fruits into very thin slices, then cut each slice into eight wedges. Cut on a plate or platter so that no juice is lost.

Combine the fruit wedges and their juice with the water in a large glass or china container. Cover, and let stand for 12 hours or overnight.

Pour the fruit mixture into a large stainless steel saucepan and bring to a rolling boil. Boil for 30 minutes. Turn off the heat, cover, and let stand for 6 hours.

Measure the fruit mixture, add an equal amount of sugar, and return to the saucepan. Bring to a boil, stirring constantly until the sugar is completely dissolved, continue to boil the marmalade, stirring occasionally, until it "sheets" from a metal spoon (see pages 112–113).

Remove from the heat, cool slightly, then ladle into manufacturer for sealing, processing, and storing.

Minute Marmalade

This is a recipe for marmalade lovers who don't have time for hours and hours of soaking, cooking, and soaking again. It takes only minutes from start to finish.

2 pink grapefruit
1½ oranges
1 lemon
1½ cups water
⅛ teaspoon baking soda
5 cups sugar
3 ounces liquid fruit pectin

Wash and sterilize seven half-pint jelly glasses, jam pots or canning jars and lids.

Wash the fruits and cut off the stem ends. Score the skin of each fruit in quarters and remove the skin. Section the fruits and set aside.

Lay the quartered fruit rinds flat. With a serrated grapefruit spoon shave off as much of the *albedo* or the white lining of the skins as possible.

Slice the rinds into very thin strips. Combine the strips with the water and the baking soda in a large stainless steel saucepan. Bring to a boil. Simmer covered for 20 minutes, stirring occasionally.

Chop the reserved fruit sections into small pieces, discarding the seeds. Add the fruit pieces to the cooked rinds and continue to cook over low heat for another 10 minutes.

Remove from the heat and measure out 3 cups. Return the measured fruit to the saucepan and stir in the sugar until completely dissolved.

Increase the heat to high, bring to a full rolling boil, stirring constantly. Boil for 1 minute, as directed on the label of the pectin package. Remove from the heat, stir in the liquid pectin, and skim off any foam that accumulates.

Continue to stir and skim for a few more minutes, then ladle into the prepared jars. Seal and process according to manufacturer's directions.

Not-So-Proper-British Marmalade

PREPARATION TIME: 10-15 MINUTES
COOKING TIME: 3-4 HOURS
YIELD: 6-8 CUPS

We always think of England in connection with marmalade, but culinary historians tell us this wonderful variety of preserves actually originated in Scotland, sometime during the 1700s. A thrifty Scot, unable to sell a consignment of very tart and bitter oranges shipped from Seville, Spain, asked his wife to see what she could do with them. The result of her labors was marmalade. Since that time, all proper British marmalade has been made with tart Seville oranges, a variety we seldom see in our supermarket produce bins. We substitute navels or Valencias for the Sevilles and add lemon in order to achieve the desired tartness. In case you can get Seville oranges, omit the lemon and increase the number of oranges to four.

3 navel or Valencia oranges
1 lemon
7 cups water
7-8 cups sugar

Wash and sterilize six to eight half-pint jelly glasses, jam pots or canning jars and lids.

Wash the fruits and cut off the stem ends. Combine the whole fruits with the water in a large saucepan and boil for 2 hours.

Remove the fruits from the cooking water and cool to room temperature. Set the cooking water aside.

Cut the cooled fruits into quarters and remove the seeds and the stringy center pith. Chop the fruits into small pieces and return to the reserved saucepan.

Measure the water in which the fruits were cooked and add enough water to make 7 cups. Pour the water over the fruit pieces and bring to a boil. Add 7 cups of the sugar, and stir constantly until completely dissolved. Test for sweetness and add more sugar if necessary.

Continue to cook, stirring occasionally, until the marmalade reaches the jelling stage (see pages 112–113). Remove from the heat, cool slightly, and ladle into the prepared jars. Seal and process according to manufacturer's directions.

Kumquat Marmalade

Kumquats are not as readily available as most other citrus fruits, so when we are able to get them, we stock up. They keep well in the refrigerator for several weeks.

4 cups whole kumquats
1 lemon
8 cups water
7-8 cups sugar

Wash and sterilize eight half-pint jelly glasses, jam pots or canning jars and lids.

Wash the kumquats and the lemon, cut off the stem ends, and combine the whole fruits with the water in a large saucepan. Boil for 2 hours.

Remove the fruits from the cooking water and cool to room temperature. Set the cooking water aside.

Cut the cooled fruits in half and remove the seeds. Chop the fruits in a food grinder or processor.

Measure the cooking water and add enough water to make 8 cups. Return the fruits and the water to the reserved saucepan and bring to a boil.

Stir in 7 cups of the sugar until completely dissolved. Turn the heat to low and cook until it has jelled (see pages 112-113). Stir occasionally to prevent sticking. Test for sweetness and add more sugar if necessary.

When the marmalade sheets, remove from the heat. Cool slightly and ladle into the prepared jars. Seal and process according to manufacturer's directions.

Minneola Marmalade

PREPARATION TIME: 10–15 MINUTES
COOKING TIME: 4–6 HOURS
YIELD: 6–7 CUPS

Minneola tangelos are some of the most distinctive of all the citrus varieties, with little knob-like projections on their stem ends. A deep orange in color, they have a pleasing taste and aroma.

4 Minneola tangelos
1 lemon
7 cups water
7-8 cups sugar

Wash and sterilize six or seven half-pint jelly glasses, jam pots or canning jars and lids.

Wash the fruits and cut off the stem ends. Combine the whole fruits in a large saucepan with the water and boil for 2 hours.

Remove the fruits from the cooking water and cool to room temperature. Set the cooking water aside.

Cut the cooled fruits into quarters, remove seeds and pith, then chop the peel and the trimmed sections into small pieces and return the pieces to the reserved saucepan.

Measure the cooking water and add enough to make 7 cups. Pour over the fruit pieces and bring to a boil. Add 7 cups of sugar, and stir constantly until completely dissolved. Test for sweetness and add more sugar if necessary.

Cook the mixture until it has jelled (see pages 112–113). Stir occasionally to prevent sticking and burning.

When the marmalade sheets, remove from the heat. Cool slightly and ladle into the prepared jars. Seal and process according to manufacturer's directions.

Orange Butter

2 large carrots
¾ cup water
1 orange
juice of 1 lemon
1 cup crushed pineapple, drained
1 cup sugar, or to taste

Wash and sterilize five or six half-pint jelly glasses, jam pots or canning jars and lids.

Wash, peel, and trim the carrots. Cut into quarters in a medium saucepan with the water and bring to a boil.

Peel the oranges, remove pith and seeds, separate into sections, and add to the carrot mixture. Reduce the heat and simmer, stirring occasionally, until the carrots are tender. Cool slightly, then blend or process to a smooth sauce. Return the sauce to the saucepan with the lemon juice, the drained pineapple, and the sugar.

Cook the mixture until it is of spreading consistency. Ladle into the prepared jars and store in the refrigerator for up to two weeks. For longer storage, seal and process the jars as you would for apple butter following manufacturer's directions.

Preserved Kumquats

4 cups kumquats
2 cups water
2½ cups sugar

Wash and sterilize six half-pint jelly glasses, jam pots or canning jars and lids. Wash the kumquats and pierce each fruit in several places with a fork or skewer. (This will prevent bursting.)

Bring the water to a boil in a large covered stainless steel saucepan, add the pierced kumquats, and simmer until tender. Remove the kumquats from the water and set aside.

Stir the sugar into the cooking water until completely dissolved, bring to a boil, and cook this syrup for 5 minutes. Return the kumquats to the saucepan and simmer for 1 hour or until they have a transparent look.

Turn off the heat, cover the saucepan, and let the fruit mixture stand overnight. In the morning, remove the kumquats and set aside. Return the syrup to a boil and cook over medium heat until thick. Return the kumquats to the saucepan and cook for 5 minutes. Ladle into the prepared jars. Seal and process according to manufacturer's directions.

Lemon Jam

1½ lemons, including peel
1 orange, including peel
1½-2 cups sugar
½ cup water
½ teaspoon cinnamon
¼ teaspoon cloves

Wash and sterilize three or four half-pint jelly glasses, jam pots or small canning jars and lids.

Wash the fruits, cut into quarters, remove the stem ends, center pith, and all seeds. Grind the trimmed fruits in a food chopper or processor. Combine the ground-up fruits in a large saucepan with 1½ cups of the sugar and the water.

Bring the mixture to a boil, reduce the heat, and simmer until it begins to thicken. Check the taste and add more sugar if necessary.

Stir in the spices and continue to simmer the jam until thick, stirring occasionally. Ladle into the prepared jars and store in the refrigerator. It should keep well for several weeks. Or, fill and seal small sterilized canning jars and process according to manufacturer's directions.

HOW TO BUY CITRUS FRUITS

When shopping for citrus fruits, remember that you needn't be concerned about ripeness: All of them are harvested ripe, as mandated by state laws and federal marketing agreements under federal statute. And don't fret too much over which variety to buy: Only an expert can distinguish among the many varieties of oranges, lemons, grapefruit, limes, and mandarins, most of which are more or less equal in quality.

Oranges

Look for firm, heavy fruit with bright, smooth skin. Very rough skin texture indicates unusually thick skin and scanty flesh. Dull dry skin and spongy texture indicate aging and diminished eating quality. Avoid oranges with cuts or skin punctures, or soft, discolored, and weakened areas of skin around the stem end or bottom button. Since harvest times vary considerably, fresh oranges are available year-round.

Grapefruit

Choose grapefruit with smooth skins, firm, round but somewhat flattened and heavy for their size. Avoid fruits with rough or wrinkled skin and pointed stem ends, flabby and springy to the touch.

The glossy look common to most grapefruit results from a waxing treatment given to prevent loss of moisture. Imperfections such as scars, scratches, and discoloration are cosmetic flaws that do not affect quality.

The red- and pink-fleshed varieties have a slight blush of pink on the rind, and some seeds. They are often sweeter and have a higher beta-carotene content than white varieties. Most white-fleshed varieties are basically seedless.

Florida grapefruit are harvested from October through July; Texas grapefruit from September through May; California and Arizona varieties from November through June or early July, and June through October.

Pummelos

Pummelos should have the same characteristics as grapefruit, though you'll find they have flesh that is firmer and less juicy than the grapefruit. They are available fresh from December through August.

Lemons

Buy lemons that have fine-textured, bright yellow unblemished skin, or those with a slight greenish tinge, heavy for their size. Avoid lightweight fruits with coarse, decidedly green skin and mold or soft spots at the stem ends, which may indicate rot at the center of the fruits. They are harvested from May through August, but are available year-round because they keep so well.

Limes

Choose limes with glossy fine-textured bright green or yellow-tinged skins. The Mexican lime is often harvested while the skin is still completely green but is not fully ripe until it yellows. Some purple or brownish mottling indicates a condition called "scald" which does not affect the flesh of the fruit. However, limes which have passed the yellowing stage and have dull brownish skins should be avoided.

Only two types of true lime are marketed in this country: The Mexican and the Bearss (sic). Both are acidic and juicy. They are harvested from June through August and are available year-round.

Mandarins

Look for firm, deep yellow or orange fruits. Because of their loose skin they may not feel firm to the touch so squeeze them carefully to test the fruit inside. Avoid pale yellow or greenish fruits with cut or punctured skins or soft spots, all of which are signs of decay. All thirteen common mandarin varieties are delicate and quite perishable, easy to peel, and seedy.

Most mandarins are grown in Florida where peak harvests are from October through March. The California harvest stretches from November through May.

Tangelos

This fruit, a cross between the tangerine and the pummelo or the tangerine and the grapefruit, should be like its parents — heavy and bright-colored, with firm, smooth skin. Do not buy those that have blemishes, soft spots or mold. They are harvested from November through April.

Tangors

Choose tangors with the same characteristics as the fruits from which it was developed — the tangerine and the orange. Avoid those with excessively loose, discolored skin, bruises, and soft spots. Tangors are harvested from late December to March and April.

Kumquats

Buy kumquats that are uniform in shape, heavy for their size, bright and glossy, with smooth, yellow-orange skins, firm but somewhat springy when pinched.

Two major varieties are harvested in this country: The oblong Nagami and the round Meiwa. Both are harvested from December through May, and are at their best in the winter months.

Citrons

The citron's thick skin is its best quality and it should be bright, smooth and firm, with a strong, fresh scent. Give it a squeeze to test it for firmness and density.

Two major varieties — the Etrog and the fingered Citron sometimes known as "Buddha's Hand" — are grown in California and Arizona. They are everbearing, but are harvested most often in the autumn. They are available in markets year-round.

HOW TO STORE CITRUS FRUITS

Citrus fruits usually go directly to a processor for juicing and/or canning, or to market for fresh produce after they are picked and graded. If for some reason the fruits have to be cold-stored in a warehouse or in transit, maximum storage time ranges from two to three weeks for mandarins, up to five or six months for lemons. The next stop for the fruits — supermarket produce bins — will probably be brief since most managers aim for a two-day "turnover" in their produce sections.

Once you get them home, there is no need to leave the fruits at room temperature to ripen, though they will stay fresh and whole for several days to two weeks: By law, citrus fruits are not picked until they are fully ripe. (An exception to the rule is the Mexican or Key lime. It is picked when it is not fully ripe. However, there is little difference between the under ripe and fully ripe fruit.)

Store the whole fruits in the crisper drawers of your refrigerator or in open containers on the shelves. Don't put them in airtight plastic bags because mold develops quickly when air can't circulate freely. Fresh juice can be kept in the refrigerator in covered containers for 2-3 days without loss of flavor or nutrients, except for the juice of navel oranges, which tends to become bitter tasting in just a few hours.

If you happen to come by a large supply of citrus fruits, you may want to store what you can't consume right away. If so, your freezer is your best bet, though *whole* citrus fruits don't freeze well: They lose moisture, suffer dry-separation of juice cells and buckling of section walls.

However, we have successfully frozen citrus fruit slices and wedges without special fuss for use later in beverages, or in dishes such as *PATATAS DULCES CON NARANJAS* (page 70). Just cut or slice the fruit to the thickness you want, layer the slices in airtight plastic bags or containers, and put them unceremoniously into the freezer. They separate easily so you can take them out as you need them, without having to thaw the whole bunch. A fancier way to do the job is to cut washed and trimmed whole oranges into cartwheels and freeze them in different sized containers of water, such as empty margarine tubs for use later in punch bowls or drinks.

Still another method is to cut lemons, limes, and oranges into paperthin slices, lay them on cookie sheets or foil, and freeze them solid. Carefully remove the frozen slices and put them in a plastic freezer bag until you need them to garnish salads, main dishes or beverages. Lemon and lime "twists" can be frozen for future use in the same way. Orange, lemon, and lime peel for use as zest can also be frozen and thawed with no loss of flavor or body.

According to the experts at the U.S. Department of Agriculture,* containers used in freezing should be easy to seal; waterproof so they won't leak; preferably made of glass, metal or rigid plastic, all of which are durable; flexible so they won't crack at low temperatures; and moisture- and vapor-proof. Waxed paper and paper cartons from cottage cheese, ice cream, and milk don't measure up.

The citrus fruits most commonly sectioned and bulk frozen are grapefruit and oranges. Here's how the USDA says to proceed:

"Select firm fruit, heavy for its size and free from soft spots. Wash and peel. Divide fruit into sections, removing all membranes and seeds. Slice your oranges if desired. For grapefruit with many seeds, cut fruit in half, remove seeds; cut or scoop out sections.

"Pack fruit into containers. Cover with cold 40 percent syrup consisting of three parts of sugar to four parts of water or excess fruit juice, or a combination of juice and water. For better quality, add one-half teaspoon crystalline ascorbic acid to a quart of syrup. Leave head space as specified below. Seal and freeze."

HEAD SPACE	Container with wide top opening:		Container with narrow top opening:	
Type of Pack	Pint	Quart	Pint	Quart
Liquid Pack (fruit packed in juice, sugar, syrup or water; crushed or puree, juice)	½"	1"	¾"	1-1½"
Dry Pack (fruit packed without added sugar or liquid)	½"	½"	½"	½"

Frozen citrus requires only thawing if it's to be served uncooked. For the best color and flavor, leave it in its sealed container while it thaws and then serve it at once. It can be thawed in the refrigerator, at room temperature, or in a pan of cold water. Allow six to eight hours on a refrigerator shelf for thawing a one-pound package of fruit packed in syrup; two to four hours at room temperature; and half an hour to an hour in a pan of cool water. Thaw only as much as you need at one time, and treat it like fresh fruit for use in recipes.

If you have leftover thawed fruit it's a good idea to use it in a cooked dish, proceeding as you would with fresh fruit. If the recipe calls for sugar, allow for any sweetening that was added before the fruit was frozen. Frozen fruits often have more juice than called for in recipes for baked products using fresh fruits, so you should drain and measure the juice before adding it to the other ingredients.

Home juice freezing is usually practical only for those who have citrus trees growing in their back yards. Follow guidelines published by the U.S. Department of Agriculture.* Lemon juice and Valencia orange juice can both be frozen for as long as four months. See USDA storage guidelines for other juices.

*For additional information, see U.S. Department of Agriculture Home & Garden Bulletin No. 10, (1982) obtainable from the U.S. Government Printing Office, Washington, D.C.

TOOLS FOR CITRUS ARTISTRY

To get the most out of citrus in the kitchen, certain basic tools are necessary. Exotic and expensive apparatus is available, but just a few are absolutely essential to get started. A visit to your kitchen specialty shop or a department store will serve your needs well and at modest expense.

Handy plastic grater is raised on one end; allows you to hold fruit firmly and scrub it with a safe, natural downward stroke — deposits flavedo bits on waxed paper underneath.

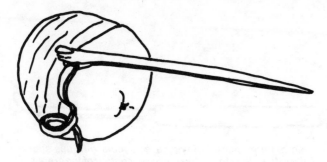

Snacker® cuts clean strips of orange, lemon, and lime peel for making decorative twists and ties.

Oranges, limes, and the larger Bearss limes surrender their juice to this plain and simple hand squeezer.

Heavy-duty juice squeezer for the cook who really means business. Pump-type handle lets you bring strong pressure to bear and extract the maximum amount of juice available.

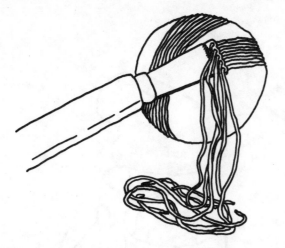

The "zester" is a unique tool custom-made for citrus. Draw the toothed tip toward you across the fruit and rake off those tangy citrus-flavored buds.

Even more grapefruit dining ease is yours with this special knife with a blade that curves to fit the contour of the grapefruit and neatly loosens the fruit around the rind rim.

For more convenient scooping of sectioned bites out of grapefruit halves, this sharp-tipped spoon with serrated edges is a must.

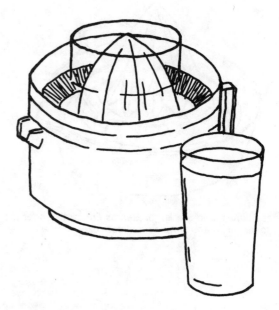

Electric juicer gets every drop out of your citrus at the touch of a button. Convenient for juicing all types of fruits.

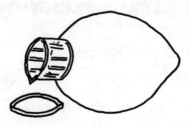

Clever spigot punches into the end of a rolled-soft fruit. Squeeze and — presto — drips and sips come forth. Pop into the refrigerator to save unused juice for later.

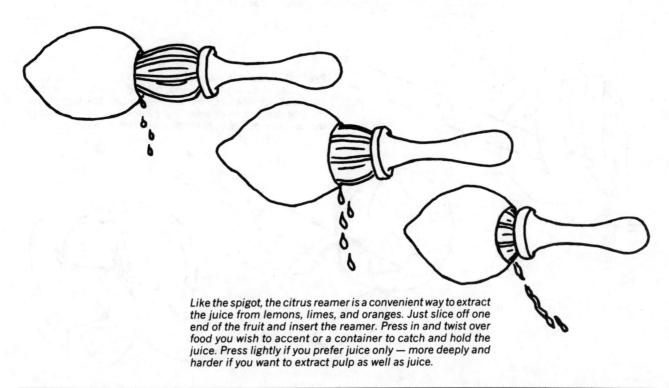

Like the spigot, the citrus reamer is a convenient way to extract the juice from lemons, limes, and oranges. Just slice off one end of the fruit and insert the reamer. Press in and twist over food you wish to accent or a container to catch and hold the juice. Press lightly if you prefer juice only — more deeply and harder if you want to extract pulp as well as juice.

SPECIAL CITRUS TECHNIQUES

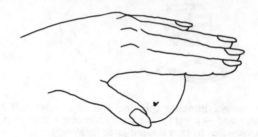

Roll 'em! More juice is freed if you get in the habit of rolling citrus fruit under the heel of your hand until soft and fruit is at room temperature.

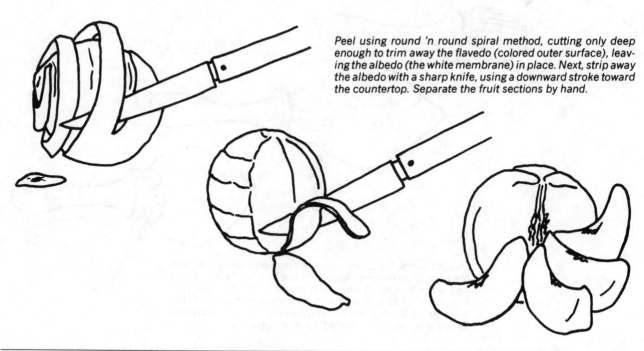

Peel using round 'n round spiral method, cutting only deep enough to trim away the flavedo (colored outer surface), leaving the albedo (the white membrane) in place. Next, strip away the albedo with a sharp knife, using a downward stroke toward the countertop. Separate the fruit sections by hand.

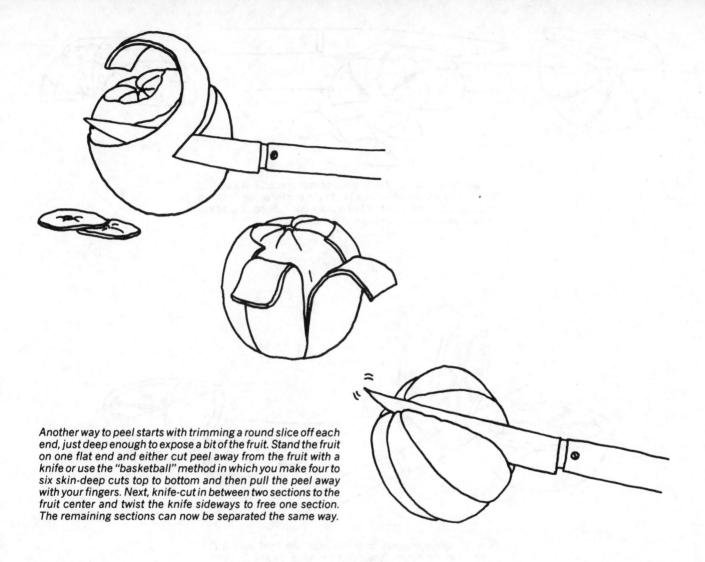

Another way to peel starts with trimming a round slice off each end, just deep enough to expose a bit of the fruit. Stand the fruit on one flat end and either cut peel away from the fruit with a knife or use the "basketball" method in which you make four to six skin-deep cuts top to bottom and then pull the peel away with your fingers. Next, knife-cut in between two sections to the fruit center and twist the knife sideways to free one section. The remaining sections can now be separated the same way.

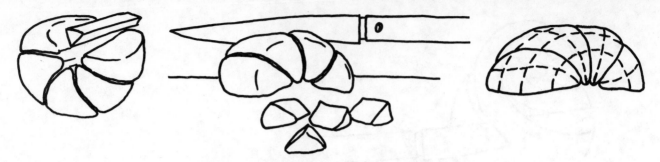

For easy preparation of bite-sized orange pieces, cut a peeled
fruit in half lengthwise. Cut a "V" to the center of the fruit and
strip out the core. Lay the two halves flat side down and cut
crisscross to the size desired.

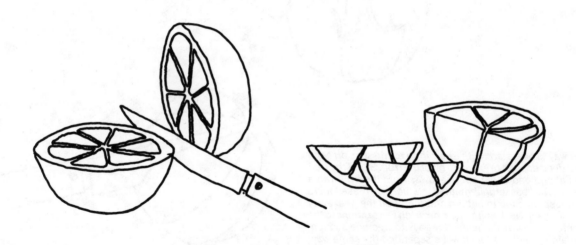

To make citrus wedges or smiles, cut the fruit across the
middle. Lay the halves face down and slice toward the center
into quarters, sixths or eighths. Decorate main dishes or serve
as breakfast or snacks.

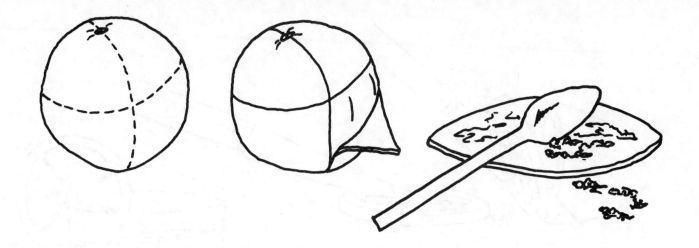

To sliver and mince peel, make two cuts around the whole fruit, lengthwise (from tip to stem and back again) to divide the peel into four quarters. As with the "basketball" peeling method, cut only deep enough to get through the albedo, but not so deep as to damage the fruit inside. Now strip peel quarters away with fingers. Place one peel quarter at a time on a cutting board and with a spoon, scrape away as much albedo as possible until only the thin flavedo remains. Cut into very thin strips and chop strips into fine bits.

Slice orange, lemon or lime crosswise into quarter-inch thicknesses. Make a knife cut on the edge of the rind and slip onto the rim of a cocktail glass, or float in a punch bowl. Also place on roasts, fish or other dishes.

Cartwheels of orange, lemon or pink grapefruit can be used purely for decoration or sprinkled with diced or sliced black olives, paprika or parsley and served with an entree. Another idea — place on a cookie and serve as a diet dessert.

SPECIAL CITRUS TREATMENTS

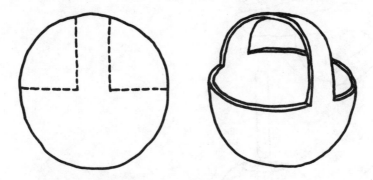

Make wedge-shaped cuts into the stem end of a grapefruit, leaving a "strap handle" across the top. Cut into the remaining fruit and carefully scoop out the pulp. Scrape the white albedo clean and dry. Fill with hors d'oeuvres.

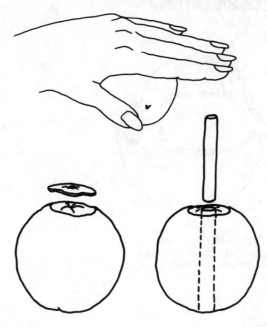

Roll-soft a grapefruit or orange. Cut a 1–1½-inch diameter slice off the fruit stem end. With a sawing motion, cut into the fruit, gradually deepening the cut around the fruit core until your knife tip touches bottom, but does not cut through it. Carefully extract the cut cylinder, including core. Trickle in the liqueur of your choice. Insert straw, chill, and serve.

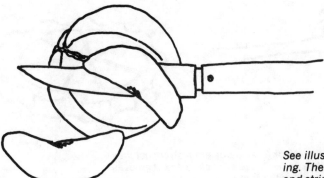

See illustration on page 129 for "basketball" method of peeling. Then loosen peel sections with fingers, remove the fruit, and strip the albedo off the skin with a spoon. Break fruit into sections, mix with shrimp, avocado slices or pimiento, and fill the shell.

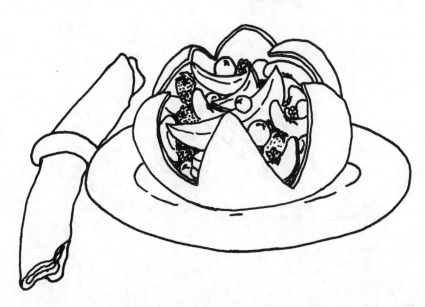

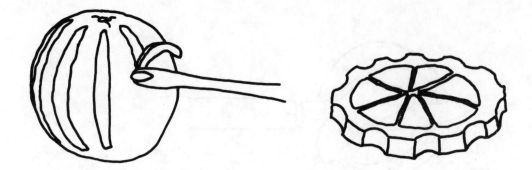

For a different cartwheel look (oranges or lemons), cut notches around the edge with a knife. Or use a Snacker® to cut grooves into the peel before slicing the fruit.

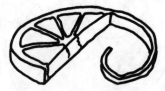

Cut a quarter section out of a cartwheel, leaving the peel as a tail. Curl the tail toward the center.

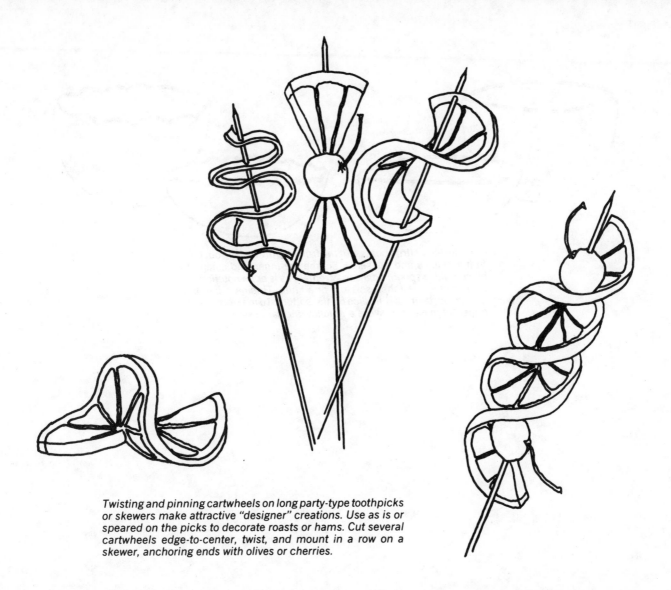

Twisting and pinning cartwheels on long party-type toothpicks or skewers make attractive "designer" creations. Use as is or speared on the picks to decorate roasts or hams. Cut several cartwheels edge-to-center, twist, and mount in a row on a skewer, anchoring ends with olives or cherries.

To make easy citrus boats, cut the fruit lengthwise. Dig out the fruit and juice and conserve. Scrape the inner rind clean of albedo with a spoon. Edges may remain as is or be notched or scalloped with kitchen scissors or a knife. Tippiness can be avoided by taking a thin slice off the bottom. To make shells or cups, cut in half crosswise and follow the same steps.

U.S. RDA (RECOMMENDED DAILY DIETARY ALLOWANCES)

(Table I)	Unit	Infants 0-12 months	Children under 4 years	Adults and children 4 or more years	Pregnant or lactating women
Vitamin A	IU	1500	2500	5000	8000
Vitamin C	mg	35	40	60	60
Folacin	mg	0.1	0.2	0.4	0.8
Thiamine (B₁)	mg	0.5	0.7	1.5	1.7
Riboflavin (B₂)	mg	0.6	0.8	1.7	2.0
Niacin	mg	8	9	20	20
Vitamin (B₆)	mg	0.4	0.7	2	2.5
Vitamin (B₁₂)	mcg	2	3	6	8
Biotin	mg	0.05	0.15	0.3	0.3
Pantothenic acid	mg	3	5	10	10

IU = International Unit   mg = milligram   mcg = microgram

The U.S. RDA system was developed by the federal Food and Drug Administration for its nutrition labeling and dietary supplement programs. Above table abstracted from the comprehensive U.S. RDA system for use in labeling of dietary supplements. It lists only pertinent vitamin requirements.

CITRUS FRUIT VITAMINS

(Table II)	Vitamin A IU	Thiamine mg	Riboflavin mg	Niacin mg	Vitamin C mg
Orange: 1, medium					
All varieties	270	.11	.05	.4	70
Orange Juice: 1 cup					
Raw, all varieties	500	.22	.07	1.0	124
Canned, unsweetened	440	.15	.07	.8	86
Frozen concentrate, diluted with 3 parts water	190	.20	.04	.5	97
Grapefruit: ½, medium					
Raw, all varieties	10*	.04	.02	.3	41
Grapefruit juice: 1 cup					
Raw, all varieties	20	.10	.05	.5	94
Canned,					
unsweetened	20	.10	.05	.6	72
sweetened	20	.10	.06	.8	67
Lemon: 1, medium	20	.02	.01	.1	31
Lemon juice: 1 cup					
Raw	50	.07	.02	.2	112
Canned or bottled unsweetened	40	.10	.02	.5	61
Lime juice: 1 cup					
Raw	20	.05	.02	.2	72
Canned, unsweetened	40	.08	.01	.4	16
Mandarin (tangerine): 1, medium					
Raw	770	.09	.02	.1	26
Canned, in light syrup, fruit and liquid	2120	.13	.11	1.1	50
Mandarin (tangerine) juice: 1 cup					
Canned, sweetened	1050	.15	.05	.2	55

*For white grapefruit; pink and red grapefruit have about 310 IU. Note: Vitamin content calculated without fruit peel, seed or membrane.

Source: "Nutritive Value of Foods," U.S. Dept. of Agriculture, 1986.

CITRUS FRUIT MINERALS

(Table III)	Calcium mg	Phosphorus mg	Iron mg	Potassium mg	Sodium mg
Orange: 1, medium					
All varieties	52	18	0.1	237	tr
Orange juice: 1 cup					
Raw, all varieties	27	42	0.5	496	2
Canned, unsweetened	20	35	1.1	436	5
Frozen, concentrate diluted with 3 parts water	22	40	0.2	473	2
Grapefruit: ½, medium					
Raw, all varieties	14	10	0.1	167	tr
Grapefruit juice: 1 cup					
Raw, all varieties	22	37	0.5	400	2
Canned,					
unsweetened	17	27	0.5	378	2
sweetened	20	28	0.9	405	5
Lemon: 1, medium	15	9	0.3	80	1
Lemon juice: 1 cup					
Raw	17	15	0.1	303	2
Canned or bottled, unsweetened	27	22	0.3	249	51*
Lime juice: 1 cup					
Raw	22	17	0.1	268	2
Canned, unsweetened*	30	25	0.6	185	39
Mandarin (tangerine):					
1 medium					
Raw	12	8	0.1	132	1
Canned, in light syrup, fruit and liquid	18	25	0.9	197	15
Mandarin (tangerine) juice: 1 cup					
Canned, sweetened	45	35	0.5	443	2

*Sodium benzoate and sodium bisulfite added as preservatives. Note: Nutrient content calculated without fruit peel, seed or membrane.

Source: USDA "Nutritive Value of Foods," 1986; and USDA Handbook No. 456, 1975.

CITRUS FRUIT FOOD VALUES

(Table IV)	Energy cal	Protein g	Fat g	Cholesterol mg	Carbohydrates g
Orange: 1, medium					
All varieties	60	1	tr	0	15
Orange juice: 1 cup					
Raw, all varieties	110	2	tr	0	26
Canned, unsweetened	105	1	tr	0	25
Frozen concentrate, diluted with 3 parts water	110	2	tr	0	27
Grapefruit: ½, medium					
Raw, all varieties	40	1	tr	0	10
Grapefruit juice: 1 cup					
Raw, all varieties	95	1	tr	0	23
Canned,					
unsweetened	95	1	tr	0	22
sweetened	115	1	tr	0	28
Lemon: 1, medium	15	1	tr	0	5
Lemon juice: 1 cup					
Raw	60	1	tr	0	21
Canned or bottled, unsweetened	50	1	1	0	16
Lime juice: 1 cup					
Raw	65	1	tr	0	22
Canned, unsweetened	50	1	1	0	16
Mandarin (tangerine): 1, medium					
Raw	35	1	tr	0	9
Canned, in light syrup fruit and liquid	155	1	tr	0	41
Mandarin (tangerine) juice: 1 cup					
Canned, sweetened	125	1	tr	0	30

Key: g = gram; mg = milligram; tr = trace
Note: Nutrient content calculated without fruit peel, seed or membrane.

Source: "Nutritive Value of Foods," U.S. Dept. of Agriculture, 1986.

A

Acorn Squash, Stuffed, 72
Albedo, 2, 3, 7, 9
Ambrosia Olympia, 19
Ambrosia Pie, 104
Appetizers
  Ambrosia Olympia, 19
  Broiled Grapefruit, 17
  Cartwheels and Cream Cheese, 19
  Chilled Spiced Fruit, 17
  Fillings (sandwich), 14
  Fresh Fruit Fondue, 16
  Grapefruit on the Half Shell, 15
  Grapefruit Puffs, 18
  Mixed Fruit Cup, 14
  Pink Cocktail, 15
  Pink Ladies, 16
  Seafood and Citrus Nests, 18
  Snack-Time Dips, 13
  Spreads, 14
Apple
  Cider, Hot Spiced, 23
  juice
      B.Y.O.B. Punch, 22
      Wassail, 23
  and Orange Bars, 89
  Simple Fruit Salad, 44
Applesauce, 9
Apricots
  Color-Me-Orange Bread, 75
  Double Dip Sauce, 93
  Tart Terrific, 103
Arizona Meatloaf, 53
"Arizona Sweet" oranges, 4
Aunt Vi's Lemon Tube Cake, 83

Avocados
  Guacamole Dressing, 48
  Salad Ring, 40
  Snack-Time Dips, 13
  Soup, 66

B

B-complex vitamins, 1. *See also* Vitamins
B.Y.O.B. Punch, 22
Bananas
  Bread, 74
  Fruit Parfait, 102
  Simple Fruit Salad, 44
  Solsken Soppa, 63
  Tart Terrific, 103
Barbecue Sauce, 60
Bars. *See also* Cookies
  Apple and Orange Bars, 89
  Nut 'n' Limey Bars, 90
  Tangerola Bars, 88
Basic Salad Dressing, 47
Bavarian Cream, 101
Beans, Baked, Florida-Style, 71
Beef
  Arizona Meatloaf, 53
  Boeuf en Marinade, 56
  Steak à la Suisse, 51
  Sweet and Citrus Tenderloin
    Tips, 54
Beets, Sweet, 72
Best Ever Jam Sauce, 95
Beta-carotene, 2, 7–8

Beverages
  B.Y.O.B. Punch, 22
  Boston Commons Punch, 25
  Café Brûlot, 22
  "Champagne," 29
  citrus milkshake, 10
  Citrus Soda, 27
  Glogg, 21
  Hot Spiced Cider, 23
  Hot Toddy, 32
  Instant Breakfast, 34
  lemonade slush, 10
  Lemonberry Punch, 24
  limeade slush, 10
  Mulled Wine, 30
  Old-Fashioned Lemonade, 28
  Orange and Egg Nog, 28
  Orange Bounce, 26
  Orange Mist, 29
  Partygoer's Punch, 24
  Provincetown Pick-Me-Up, 31
  Side Lines Soda, 30
  Sonnenobst Shake, 25
  Sunday Punch, 26
  Tangerine Crush, 27
  Tangerorange Milk Shake, 28
  Thousand Lakes Fizz, 27
  Wassail, 23
Black Walnut Bread, 77
Boeuf en Marinade, 56
Boiled Dressing, 47
Boston Commons Punch, 25
Bouquet oranges, 4
Brandy and Orange Sauce, 94

Bread. *See also* Muffins; Toast
  Banana, 74
  Black Walnut, 77
  Color-Me-Orange, 75
  Honey Nut, 76
  Limey Loaf, 73
  Orange Raisin, 74
Breakfast. *See* Brunch
Bride's Cookbook Orange Frosting, 96
Broiled Grapefruit, 17
Brunch
  Cartwheels Mac Muffin, 37
  Cinnamon and Citrus Toast, 35
  French Toast with Orange Sauce, 36
  Fruit in Batter, 35
  Instant Breakfast, 34
  Muesli Our Way, 34
  Omelette Orange, 33
  Starters, 36
  Toast with a Twist, 37
  Waffle Toppers, 38
Buddha's Hand (citron), 6, 122
Butter Cream Frosting, Grapefruit, 97
Buttermilk, 9
  Soup, Hot, Great Aunt Vic's, 67

C

Cabbage, Cool Slaw, 41
Café Brûlot, 22
Cake. *See also* Coffeecake
  Aunt Vi's Lemon Tube, 83
  Downside-Up, 82
  Grapefruit Chiffon, 81
  Lemon Torte, 84
  Orange Nut, 85
California Custard, 110
California Rice, 68
Cancer, 1, 2
Candied citron peel, 8
Candied Fruit Muffins, 77

Carrots
  Bake, Orange, 69
  Mother's Sunshine, 68
  Orange Butter, 118
  Oranged, a la Holtville, 71
  Pudding, 109
  Soup, Orange, 65
Cartwheels and Cream Cheese, 19
Cartwheels Mac Muffin, 37
Casserole, More-Than-Tuna, 49
"Champagne," 29
Chandler pummelos, 4
Chicken
  and Citrus Sandwich, 50
  Ensalada de Pollo con Queso, 58
  Lemon-Fried, 59
  Mac Orange, 50
  Saucy Baked, 52
Chilled Spiced Fruit, 17
Chinotto oranges, 4
Cholesterol, 3, 7
Cider, Hot Spiced, 23
Cinnamon and Citrus Toast, 35
Citrons, 8. *See also* Citrus fruits
  buying tips, 122
  Candied Fruit Muffins, 77
  peel, candied, 8
  varieties, 6, 122
Citrus fruits, 6-8, 128-131. *See also*
    specific fruits
  boats, 138
  buying tips, 121-122
  cartwheels, 132, 136
  food values, 142
  freezing, 123-124
  juice. *See* Juice
  milkshake, 10
  nutritional value of, 1-3, 6-8, 11,
    40-142
  peel, 9, 11, 128-129
    drying, 10
    slivered and minced, 131

Soda, 27
special treatments, 132-138
storing, 122-124
tools for, 124-127
"tree" centerpiece, 9
types of, 3-6
wedges, 130
Clementine mandarins, 5
Coffeecake, Grapefruit, 79
Collagen, 1
Colon cancer, 2
Color-Me-Orange Bread, 75
Cookies. *See also* Bars
  Lemon Wafers, 86
  Lemonut Balls, 87
  Pennies-From-Heaven, 91
  Treasure Chest, 87
Cooking tips, 9-11
Cool Slaw, 41
Copper, destruction of vitamin C
  and, 9
Crab, Seafood and Citrus Nests, 18
Cranberries, Right On! Relish, 70
Cream Cheese
  Cartwheels and, 19
  Frosting, Pink, 96
Crisp, Mincemeat, 108
Curried Citrus Dressing, 46
Custard, California, 110

D

Dancy mandarins, 5
Dancy, G.L., 5
Dates, Muffins Tangier, 79
"Degreening" oranges, 7
Dessert. *See also* Bars; Cake; Cookies;
  Pie
  Bavarian Cream, 101
  California Custard, 110
  Carrot Pudding, 109
  Frozen Calico Cream, 100

frozen orange treats, 10
Fruit Parfait, 102
ideas, 9–10
Lime Marble, 108
Mincemeat Crisp, 108
Mousse à l'Orange, 102
Orange Pattipans, 105
Oranges Ganymede, 98
sauce. *See also* Frosting
    Best Ever Jam, 95
    Brandy and Orange, 94
    Double Dip, 93
    Light Lemon, 95
    Orange, 93
Tangerine Sorbet, 99
Tart Terrific, 103
"Diet, Nutrition and Cancer," 1
Diller oranges, 4
Dip, Snack-Time, 13
Double Dip Sauce, 93
Downside-Up Cake, 82
Dressing. *See* Salad dressing
Drinks. *See* Beverages
Duncan grapefruit, 4
Dweet tangors, 5–6

E

Egg Nog, Orange and, 28
Eggs
    French Toast with Orange Sauce, 36
    Instant Breakfast, 34
    Omelette Orange, 33
    Orange and Egg Nog, 28
    Toast with a Twist, 37
Ensalada de Pollo con Queso, 58
Entrées
    Arizona Meatloaf, 53
    Boeuf en Marinade, 56
    Chicken and Citrus Sandwich, 50
    Chicken Mac Orange, 50
    Ensalada de Pollo con Queso, 58

Jambon au Vin Blanc, 55
Lemon-Fried Chicken, 59
More-Than-Tuna Casserole, 49
Poached Red Snapper, 57
Salmon Mousse, 57
Saucy Baked Chicken, 52
Steak à la Suisse, 51
Sweet and Citrus Tenderloin
    Tips, 54
Turkey Delight, 53
Etrog (citron), 6, 122
Eureka lemons, 5

F

Fiber, 2
Fillings (sandwich), 14
Fingered citron, 6, 122
Fish
    More-Than-Tuna Casserole, 49
    Poached Red Snapper, 57
    Salad, Our Favorite, 43
    Salmon Mousse, 57
Flavedo, 9, 11
Florida, juice produced by, 7
Florida-Style Baked Beans, 71
Folacin, 1
Folic acid, 7
Fondue
    Fourth of July, 94
    Fresh Fruit, 16
Fourth of July Fondue, 94
Freezing, 123–124
French Toast with Orange Sauce, 36
Fresh Fruit Dressing, 46
Fresh Fruit Fondue, 16
Fritters, Fruit in Batter, 35
Frosting
    Bride's Cookbook Orange, 96
    Grapefruit Butter Cream, 97
    Lemon Glaze, 97
    Orange Glaze, 97

Pink Cream Cheese, 96
Sour Cream, 96
Frozen Calico Cream, 100
Frozen Fruit Salad, 41
Frozen orange treats, 10
Fruchte in Backteig, 35
Fruit in Batter, 35
Fruit Parfait, 102

G

Gelatin, Made-From-Scratch, 44
Glaze. *See* Frosting
Glogg, 21
Grapefruit. *See also* Citrus fruits
    Avocado Salad Ring, 40
    Avocado Soup, 66
    Broiled, 17
    Butter Cream Frosting, 97
    buying tips, 121
    cartwheels, 132
    carving for hallowe'en, 9
    "Champagne," 29
    Chiffon Cake, 81
    Citrus Soda, 27
    Coffeecake, 79
    dessert idea, 10
    Ensalada de Pollo con Queso, 58
    Fruit in Batter, 35
    knife, 126
    Lovers' Marmalade, 112–113
    Made-From-Scratch Gelatin, 44
    Mellow Yellow Marmalade, 111
    Minute Marmalade, 114
    on the Half Shell, 15
    Pink Cocktail, 15
    Pink Cream Cheese Frosting, 96
    Pink Ladies, 16
    Puffs, 18
    Seafood and Citrus Nests, 18
    spoon, 126
    Starters, 36

Steak a la Suisse, 51
varieties, 4, 121
yields, 10
Grapes, Mixed Fruit Cup, 14
Grater, 124
Great Aunt Vic's Hot Buttermilk
      Soup, 67
Guacamole Dressing, 48

H

Ham
   Jambon au Vin Blanc, 55
   Starters, 36
Hamlin oranges, 4
High blood pressure, 2
Highland Flings, 76
Honey and Orange Dressing, 47
Honey Nut Bread, 76
Hot Spiced Cider, 23
Hot Toddy, 32
Hypertension, 2

I

Ice cream. *See also* Sorbet
   Citrus milkshake, 10
   Sonnenobst Shake, 25
   topping, 9
Instant Breakfast, 34
Iron, 1, 2

J

Jam, Lemon, 120
Jambon au Vin Blanc, 55
Jelled Dressing, 48
Juice, 7, 11. *See also* specific fruits
   storage, 123, 124
Juicer, 125
   electric, 126

K

Key Lime Pie, 104
Kiwifruit
   Fruit Parfait, 102
   Tart Terrific, 103
Kumquats. *See also* Citrus fruits
   buying tips, 122
   dessert idea, 10
   Marmalade, 116
   nutritional content, 8
   Preserved, 119
   varieties, 5, 122

L

Lemonade slush, 10
Lemonberry Punch, 24
Lemondaise Sauce, 61
Lemonnaise, 45
Lemons, 8. *See also* Citrus fruits
   Barbecue Sauce, 60
   Basic Salad Dressing, 47
   Best Ever Jam Sauce, 95
   blossom, 8
   Boston Commons Punch, 25
   Butter Sauce, 59
   buying tips, 121
   cartwheels, 132, 136
   as deodorizers, 10
   -Fried chicken, 59
   Glaze, 97
   Guacamole Dressing, 48
   Jam, 120
   Jambon au Vin Blanc, 55
   juice, 9, 11
   Kumquat Marmalade, 116
   lemonade slush, 10
   Lemonberry Punch, 24
   Lemondaise Sauce, 61
   Lemonnaise, 45
   Lemonut Balls, 87
   Lovers' Marmalade, 112–113

Mellow Yellow Marmalade, 111
Meringue Pie, Mother's, 107
Minute Marmalade, 114
Mixed Citrus Marmalade, 113
More-Than-Tuna Casserole, 49
Not-So-Proper-British Marma-
      lade, 115
nutritional content, 8, 140–142
Old-Fashioned Lemonade, 28
Orange Butter, 118
Poached Red Snapper, 57
pomander balls, 11
Sauce, Light, 95
storage life, 8
Summer Soup, 64
sweet, 5
Torte, 84
Tube Cake, Aunt Vi's, 83
varieties, 5
Wafers, 86
yields, 10
Lemon-Fried Chicken, 59
Lemonut Balls, 87
Light Lemon Sauce, 95
Limeade slush, 10
Limes, 8, 11. *See also* Citrus fruits
   buying tips, 121–122
   Key, Pie, 104
   juice, 9, 11
   limeade slush, 10
   Limey Loaf, 73
   Marble, 108
   Mixed Citrus Marmalade, 113
   Nut 'n' Limey Bars, 90
   nutritional content, 8, 140–142
   Side Lines Soda, 30
   Soup, Mrs. Moore's, 65
   varieties, 5, 121–122
Limey Loaf, 73
Lisbon lemons, 5
Lovers' Marmalade, 112–113

M

Made-From-Scratch Gelatin, 44
Mandarins. *See also* Citrus fruits
buying tips, 122
Cool Slaw, 41
Downside-Up Cake, 82
Frozen Calico Cream, 100
Frozen Fruit Salad, 41
Fruit Parfait, 102
Mixed Fruit Cup, 14
nutritional content, 8, 140–142
Orange Pattipans, 105
Our Favorite Tuna Salad, 43
"Royal." *See* Tangors
Set Salad, 43
Shrimp Salad, 42
Simple Fruit Salad, 44
Tart Terrific, 103
varieties, 5
Marmalade
Kumquat, 116
Lovers', 112–113
Mellow Yellow, 111
Minute, 114
Mixed Citrus, 113
Not-So-Proper-British, 115
Marrs oranges, 4
Marsh seedless grapefruit, 4
Meatloaf, Arizona, 53
Meiwa kumquat, 122
Mellow Yellow Marmalade, 111
Milk, sour, making, 9
Milkshake
Citrus, 10
Sonnenobst, 25
Tangerorange, 28
Mincemeat Crisp, 108
Minerals, 2, 6, 8, 141
Minneola Marmalade, 117
Minneola tangelos, 5
Minute Marmalade, 114

Minute-Mix, 75
Mixed Citrus Marmalade, 113
Mixed Fruit Cup, 14
More-Than-Tuna Casserole, 49
Mother's Lemon Meringue Pie, 107
Mother's Sunshine Carrots, 68
Mousse à l'Orange, 102
Mrs. Moore's Lime Soup, 65
Muesli Our Way, 34
Muffins
Candied Fruit, 77
Highland Flings, 76
Orange, 78
Petit Pain, 78
Tangier, 79
Mulled Wine, 30

N

Nagami kumquat, 122
National Academy of Science, RDA for
adults, 7
National Cancer Institute, recom-
mendations on diet, 2
National Institute of Health, 2
National Research Council
"Diet, Nutrition and Cancer," 1
recommendations on diet, 2
Navel oranges, 4
juice, 123
Not-So-Proper-British Marma-
lade, 115
Niacin, 1
Not-So-Proper-British Marmalade, 115
Nut 'n' Limey Bars, 90
"Nutrient density," 1

O

Old-Fashioned Lemonade, 28
Omelette orange, 33
Oranged Carrots a la Holtville, 71

Oranges. *See also* Citrus fruits
Ambrosia Olympia, 19
Ambrosia Pie, 104
artificially colored, 7
Avocado Salad Ring, 4
B.Y.O.B. Punch, 22
Banana Bread, 74
Bars, Apple and, 89
Bavarian Cream, 101
Best Ever Jam Sauce, 95
Boeuf en Marinade, 56
Boiled Dressing, 47
Boston Commons Punch, 25
Bounce, 26
Butter, 118
buying tips, 121
California Rice, 68
Carrot Bake, 69
Carrot Pudding, 109
Carrot Soup, 65
cartwheels, 132, 136
Cartwheels and Cream Cheese, 19
Cartwheels Mac Muffin, 37
carving for hallowe'en, 9
"Champagne," 29
Chicken Mac Orange, 50
Chilled Spiced Fruit, 17
Color-Me-Orange Bread, 75
dessert ideas, 9–10
Dressing, 45
and Egg Nog, 28
Florida-Style Baked Beans, 71
Fresh Fruit Fondue, 16
Frosting, Bride's Cookbook, 96
frozen treats, 10
Fruit in Batter, 35
Ganymede, 98
Glaze, 97
green skin, 6–7
Highland Flings, 76
Honey and Orange Dressing, 47

Honey Nut Bread, 76
Instant Breakfast, 34
Jelled Dressing, 48
Lemon Jam, 120
Lovers' Marmalade, 112–113
Made-From-Scratch Gelatin, 44
Minute Marmalade, 114
Mist, 29
Mixed Citrus Marmalade, 113
Mousse à l'Orange, 102
Muffins, 78
Not-So-Proper British Marmalade, 115
Nut Cake, 85
nutritional content, 140–142
Omelette Orange, 33
Oranged Carrots à la Holtville, 71
Overnight Soup, 66
Partygoer's Punch, 24
Patatas Dulces con Naranjas, 70
Pattipans, 105
Petit Pain, 78
pomander balls, 11
preparing bite-sized pieces, 130
Raisin Bread, 74
ripeness, 6–7
Salad Nests, 42
Sauce, French Toast with, 36, 93
Sauce, Brandy and, 94
Shrimp Salad, 42
Simple Fruit Salad, 44
Solsken Soppa, 63
Sopa de Naranjas, 67
sour, varieties, 4
Stuffed Acorn Squash, 72
Sweet Beets, 72
Tangerine Crush, 27
Tangerorange Milk Shake, 28
"Temple." *See* Tangors
Treasure Chest Cookies, 87
varieties, 4

Waffle Toppers, 38
yields, 10
Orlando tangelos, 5
Our Favorite Tuna Salad, 43
Overnight Soup, 66

P

Pantothenic acid, 1
Parfait, Fruit, 102
Parson Brown oranges, 4
Partygoer's Punch, 24
Patatas Dulces con Naranjas, 70
Pauling, Linus, 1
Peaches
    Frozen Calico Cream, 100
    Tart Terrific, 103
Pears
    Frozen Calico Cream, 100
    Tart Terrific, 103
Peel, 9–11
Pennies-From-Heaven Cookies, 91
Perfect Potato Salad, 40
Petit Pain, 78
Pie
    Ambrosia, 104
    Crust, River Inn, 106
    Key Lime, 104
    Mother's Lemon Meringue, 107
Pineapple
    Boiled Dressing, 47
    Frozen Fruit Salad, 41
    Mellow Yellow Marmalade, 111
    Mixed Fruit Cup, 14
    Orange Butter, 118
    Set Salad, 43
    Shrimp Salad, 42
    Solsken Soppa, 63
    Tart Terrific, 103
Pineapple oranges, 4
Pink Cocktail, 15

Pink Cream Cheese Frosting, 96
Pink Ladies, 16
Poached Red Snapper, 57
Pomander balls, 11
Pomelo. *See* Pummelos
Potage au Vin, 64
Potassium, 2
Potato Salad, Perfect, 40
Preserved Kumquats, 119
Provincetown Pick-Me-Up, 31
Pudding
    Carrot, 109
    Lime Marble, 108
Pummelos, 11. *See also* Citrus fruits
    Avocado Soup, 66
    buying tips, 121
    carving for hallowe'en, 9
    ripening, 8
    varieties, 4
Punch. *See* Beverages

R

Raisin Bread, Orange, 74
Raspberries
    Best Ever Jam Sauce, 95
    Lemonberry Punch, 24
    Overnight Soup, 66
Reamer, 127
Recommended Daily Dietary Allowance (RDA) guidelines, 3, 7, 139
Red blood cells, 1
Red Snapper, Poached, 57
Reinking pummelos, 4
Riboflavin, 1
Rice, California, 68
Right On! Relish, 70
The Right Stuffing, Revisited, 69
Rind. *See* Peel
River Inn Pie Crust, 106
Roquefort Ring-Around, 39
"Royal Mandarin." *See* Tangors

S

Salad
　Cool Slaw, 41
　dressing
　　Basic, 47
　　Boiled, 47
　　Curried Citrus, 46
　　Fresh Fruit, 46
　　Guacamole, 48
　　Honey and Orange, 47
　　Jelled, 48
　　Lemonnaise, 45
　　Orange, 45
Ensalada de Pollo con Queso, 58
Frozen Fruit, 41
Nests, 42
　Our Favorite Tuna, 43
　Perfect Potato, 40
　Ring, Avocado, 40
　Roquefort Ring-Around, 39
　Set, 43
　Shrimp, 42
　Simple Fruit, 44
Salmon Mousse, 57
Salt substitute, 2-3, 6, 11
Sampson tangelos, 5
Sandwich
　Cartwheels Mac Muffin, 37
　Chicken and Citrus, 50
　Fillings, 14
Sauce. *See also* Dessert, sauce
　Barbecue, 60
　Lemon Butter, 59
　Lemondaise, 61
　Sweet and Sour, 60
Saucy Baked Chicken, 52
Seafood and Citrus Nests, 18
Seminole tangelos, 5
Set Salad, 43

Seville oranges, 4
　Not-So-Proper-British Marmalade, 115
Shrimp
　Pink Cocktail, 15
　Salad, 42
Side dishes
　California Rice, 68
　Florida-Style Baked Beans, 71
　Mother's Sunshine Carrots, 68
　Orange Carrot Bake, 69
　Oranged Carrots à la Holtville, 71
　Patatas Dulces con Naranjas, 70
　Right on! Relish, 70
　The Right Stuffing, Revisited, 69
　Stuffed Acorn Squash, 72
　Sweet Beets, 72
Side Lines Soda, 30
Simple Fruit Salad, 44
Snack-Time Dips, 13
Snacker®, 125
Snacks. *See* Appetizers
Sodium, 2-3, 6, 7, 11
Solsken Soppa, 63
Sonnenobst Shake, 25
Sopa de Naranjas, 67
Sorbet, Tangerine, 99
Soup
　Avocado, 66
　Great Aunt Vic's Hot Buttermilk, 67
　Mrs. Moore's Lime, 65
　Orange Carrot, 65
　Overnight, 66
　Potage au Vin, 64
　Solsken Soppa, 63
　Sopa de Naranjas, 67
　Summer, 64
Sour Cream Frosting, 96
Sour milk, making, 9
Spreads, 14
Spigot, 127
Starters, 36

Steak à la Suisse, 51
Storing citrus fruits, 122-124
Stuffed Acorn Squash, 72
Stuffing, The Right, Revisited, 69
Summer Soup, 64
Sunday Punch, 26
Sweet and Citrus Tenderloin Tips, 54
Sweet and Sour Sauce, 60
Sweet Beets, 72
Sweet potatoes, *Patatas Dulces con Naranjas*, 70

T

Tangelos. *See also* Citrus fruits
　Bavarian Cream, 101
　buying tips, 122
　Minneola Marmalade, 117
　Turkey Delight, 53
　varieties, 5
Tangerines. *See also* Mandarins
　Bavarian Cream, 101
　Crush, 27
　Fruit in Batter, 35
　Fruit Parfait, 102
　grating peel of, 10
　Made-From-Scratch Gelatin, 44
　Mixed Citrus Marmalade, 113
　Muffins Tangier, 79
　nutritional content, 8, 140-142
　Right On! Relish, 70
　Shrimp Salad, 42
　Simple Fruit Salad, 44
　Solsken Soppa, 63
　Sorbet, 99
　Sweet and Sour Sauce, 60
　Tangerola Bars, 88
　Tangerorange Milk Shake, 28
　Tart Terrific, 103
　The Right Stuffing, Revisited, 69
Tangerola Bars, 88
Tangerorange Milk Shake, 28

Tangors. *See also* Citrus fruits
  Bavarian Cream, 101
  buying tips, 122
  Solsken Soppa, 63
  varieties, 5–6
Tart Terrific, 103
"Temple Orange." *See* Tangors
Temple tangors, 5
Thiamine, 1
Thousand Lakes Fizz, 27
Toast
  Cinnamon and Citrus, 35
  French, with Orange Sauce, 36
  with a Twist, 37
Toppings
  Ice Cream, 9
  Waffle Toppers, 38
Torte, Lemon, 84. *See also* Cake
Treasure Chest Cookies, 87
Tuna
  More-Than-, Casserole, 49
  Salad, Our Favorite, 43
Turkey Delight, 53

U

U.S. Dept. of Agriculture guidelines
    for freezing citrus fruits, 123–124
U.S. Food and Drug Administration,
  RDA guidelines, 3, 7, 139

V

Valencia oranges, 4
  Not-So-Proper-British Marma-
    lade, 115
Vitamins, 140
  A, 2, 7
  B_{12}, 1
  B_6, 1
  C, 1, 6, 7, 9, 11

W

Wafers, Lemon, 86
Waffle Toppers, 38
Washington navel oranges, 4
  juice, 123
  Not-So-Proper-British Marma-
    lade, 115

Wassail, 23
Wine, Mulled, 30
White blood cells, 1

Y

Yams, *Patatas Dulces con Naranjas,* 70

Z

Zester, 126

Audra and Jack Hendrickson are both writers, journalists, and photographers. Their first cookbook, *The Carrot Cookbook,* Garden Way Publishing, 1987, launched them into writing a trilogy of healthful cookbooks. *Surprising Citrus* is the second in the trilogy.

They lecture and write about a wide range of subjects, but nutritious food and how to prepare it are favorite topics of their work and research. They spend most of the year in Bicknell, Utah, but winter in Birmingham, Michigan.

OTHER
GARDEN WAY PUBLISHING BOOKS
YOU WILL ENJOY

The Apple Cookbook, by Olwen Woodier. 156 pages, $10.95

The Carrot Cookbook, by Audra and Jack Hendrickson. 171 pages, $6.95

Cooking for Someone Special — Yourself, by Nancy Creech. 204 pages, $7.95

Corn: Meals and More, by Olwen Woodier. 176 pages, $6.95

The Elegant Onion, by Betty Cavage. 160 pages, $6.95

Fruits and Berries for the Home Garden, by Lewis Hill. 272 pages, $8.95

Glorious Garlic, by Charlene Braida. 192 pages, $6.95

Home Gardener's Month-by-Month Cookbook, by Marjorie Page Blanchard. 208 pages, $6.95

It's the Berries!, by Liz Anton and Beth Dooley. 144 pages, $7.95

The Joy of Gardening Cookbook, by Janet Ballantyne. 336 pages, $17.95

The No-Time-To-Cook Book, by Janet Chadwick. 160 pages, $6.95

The Power of Pasta, by Olwen Woodier. 160 pages, $6.95

The Search for the Perfect Chocolate Chip Cookie, by Gwen Steege. 144 pages, $7.95

Seasonal Salads from Around the World, by David Scott and Paddy Byrne. 152 pages, $6.95

Simply Strawberries, by Sara Pitzer. 123 pages, $6.95

Zucchini Cookbook, by Nancy C. Ralston and Marynor Jordan. 142 pages, $5.95

These books are available at your bookstore, farm store, garden center, or directly from Garden Way Publishing, Dept. 8600, Schoolhouse Road, Pownal, Vermont 05261. Please enclose $2.00 for Fourth Class or $3.00 for U.P.S. per order to cover postage and handling.